D0623301

THE AFRICAN LION
AS MAN-EATER

BY GUY COHELEACH

DELUXE LIMITED EDITION

282 /650

To Barbara — Thanks so much for your friendship and hospitality in Scotland and at Brooks Lake. All the very best

Pam & Guy Coheleach

Panther Press

This limited edition is distributed
exclusively be Trophy Room Books
Box 3041 Agoura, CA 91301
818-889-2469

email: info@trophyroombooks.com

www.trophyroombooks.com

THE AFRICAN LION
AS MAN-EATER

Researched, Written & Illustrated by Guy Coheleach
with generous contributions from friends and associates

DEDICATION

To those poor souls who have involuntarily fed lions.

In Africa, the gazelle knows it must run faster than the lion or it will be eaten.

The lion knows it must run faster than the gazelle or it will starve.

Whether you are the lion or the gazelle, you'd better be able to run fast, very fast.

If you or I see the lion he will simply walk away after satisfying his curiosity,

because he is not hunting. If he were, you would never see him.

Acknowledgments

I don't think anyone could write a serious book on lions without mentioning George Schaller's landmark work, *The Serengeti Lion*. It is referred to in every lion book I have read that was published after 1972, when *The Serengeti Lion* came out. George Schaller was very generous, gracious, and helpful, and guided me to some newer works on lions. Delia and Mark Owens, also, were just as helpful. Rather than paraphrase them, I used direct quotes from the Owenses on more important areas of their contributions.

Fiona Capstick very generously sent me copies of newspaper clippings on lion stories. She and her husband, Peter, had been collecting them for a book he would never write. He died much too soon. Craig Packer's *Into Africa* was very informative and helpful. This work on the lions of the Ngorgoro crater in Tanzania is a great comparison with the lions of the Serengeti.

Because of his vast knowledge of the publishing business Robert Vernon was immensely important in organizing the book. Design Consultant Marla Brenner's tasteful touch was most essential. I am very grateful to Rebecca Tavernini, whose incredible memory and ruthless editing make this book readable.

The book would be very bare without the input from the many professional hunters and biologists who were so kind with their stories. People like John Dugmore, John Lawrence, Mike and Fred Bartlett, Pat Hepburn, Tony Henley, Peter Capstick, Don Zaidle, Lloyd Wilmot, Pat and Heather Carr Hartley, Josep Marcon, Tony Dyer, Norman Carr, Brian Herne, John Northcote, Bill Winter, Peter Davey, Lionel Hartley, and Bill York. To the great zoologists William Conway, Jeanne Minor, Ed Maruska, Mike Kinsey, and Michael Dee go very deserved thanks. No book on man-eating lions is complete without grateful credit to George Rushby, Colonel J. H. Patterson, and C. Guggisburg.

I especially want to thank Eric Balson, whose intrepid professional hunter's ethic saved my fat butt from that so foolishly provoked elephant. Without him I would be a dried blood stain on the Luangwa River sand.

Last but far from least, I am indebted to the great golfer Jack Nicklaus for his very generous foreword and kindness through the years. I can't even imagine reaching such a peak in so competitive a sport while at the same time being such a devoted "family man." When other golfers were relaxing or preparing for the next day's game he was often flying home to one of the children's functions. That is the Jack Nicklaus that I admire and respect so much.

And I did not know he was such a good painter either.

TABLE OF CONTENTS

FOREWORD

Guy Coheleach has been a friend of mine for at least thirty years; I have been an avid collector of his artwork for as long as I can remember. What began as a business acquaintance quickly developed into a friendship rooted in our mutual interest in hunting and big game.

Guy is an amazingly diverse artist, meticulous in creating an authentic environment for his subject and a master at reproducing nuances of natural light to illuminate the scene. I am fascinated above all by Guy's extraordinary ability to capture the animals themselves—particularly lions—exactly as they would look if you came upon them in the wild. It's a tremendous talent that I think must emanate from the way he studies not just their anatomy, but also their habits, how they move, how they hunt, live, and die. He takes the time to try to know his subjects, as much as any of us can ever hope to peer into the minds of the magnificent creatures he paints.

Having hunted with Guy in Africa, I am well aware of his fascination with the African lion. But of all the great stories we've shared around the campsite with guides and trackers, none, I think, are more interesting than the accounts Guy has assembled here about the lion as hunter and killer—and, yes, as man-eater. Grisly stuff at times; eloquent at others. Guy captivates his audience with his pen almost as skillfully as he does with his incredible paintings, which bring these majestic predators to life. He is a man of tremendous talent.

By the way, if you're wondering whether we've ever played golf together...we have indeed, and I think the less I comment about that, the better. Let's just say that he plays golf about as well as I paint!

I know you will find *The African Lion As Man-Eater* a visual delight and a great read.

JACK NICKLAUS, NORTH PALM BEACH, FLORIDA

Lion Eyes, Oil on Canvas

INTRODUCTION

When a major art publisher asked me to do an art book on the lion I was very pleased. The editor suggested I also do the text. Well, since I thought I knew everything there needs to be known about this wonderful animal, I promptly agreed. Then in doing some casual reading (so I could say that I researched the book), I found out how little I really did know about lions. I very quickly realized that I wanted to fill a book with this information and not make it an art book at all. Everyone advised, however, that it would be much more successful if it had at least some of my artwork in it. Who would buy a book of only text from an artist?

So. The following pages are filled with what I think is some very interesting information about lions in both art and text. The art is my interpretation of these great animals and their neighbors. There are some old paintings and some very new paintings; some are loose, painterly pieces, while others are very tightly drawn works with a lot of detail; some have quiet moods, others have plenty of action and tension. There are little watercolor sketches and simple pencil drawings. All are my visual interpretations of this magnificent cat in its environment. I hope you will enjoy them.

These pages also are filled with my impressions of the African lion in words. Many of the incidents in this book are gathered from conversations at African campfires with some of the great veterans of the bush and some from research scientists in museums and universities as well as those in the field. Many others, of course, are from some of the great writers on Africa. Then there are my own fortunate experiences spending hundreds of beautiful days and magical nights in this incredible land. The lion is a splendid animal that leaves many different impressions on us. It is seen by many as a big, beautiful, peaceful cat, and a lounging lion is certainly about as peaceful a sight in the animal world as we can imagine. But lions live a life that at times is extremely violent, and lions eat from a very different menu than we do. I think that we are on that menu more than the tourist agencies would like us to believe.

Some people I know focus on the gentle lion, while others see its ferocious side. Some see both the patient parent tolerating its tail being the constant prey of playful cubs, and the hunting lion violently killing and feeding. If there is an emphasis in this book on the violent aspects of lions, it is because they have left an indelible, fascinating impression on me. It is also to show another side of this animal to people who forget that the lion is a predator, and a very big one. Lions kill to eat and are very good at it. While this may be the only aspect of lions covered in pulp magazines, it is not at all apparent in most media coverage that we currently see on the lion.

In my work I have had the good fortune to see Africa many times. For most of those years I was under the impression that no one had ever been harmed by lions in game parks, especially if they stayed within their vehicle. When I started this book, however, someone told me that in one year in East Africa, in the 1970s, no fewer than thirteen people were taken out of vehicles and killed by lions! That was one hell of a frightening statistic for me to hear. I have never obtained hard data to document that statement, but I did come upon enough incidents to ensure that I will not be as casual on future safaris as I have been in the past. I have left many killing stories out of this book, but wanted to include enough to leave you with the impression I was left with: The lion is a wonderful but very, very dangerous animal.

I am an artist, not a scientist. Scientists have strict rules and procedures that they must abide by in describing their subjects. You will see in this text how reluctant some are to attribute human feelings to lions, or to any other animal for that matter. I, on the other hand, find no problem in saying that lions hate hyenas, that otters enjoy themselves on a snow slide, or that my pet golden retriever is happy when vigorously wagging its tail. It is easier for me to communicate to the reader in this way. I want the information in this book to be as accurate as possible. That is why there are many quotes. I have also tried to give proper credit to the right people.

Come share with me, then some of these experiences, both mine and other's and if it is weighted too much on the scientific for some or too much on the the emotional for others, I apologize, but then again, this book is my interpretation. It is how I see the African lion.

Arthur, Oil on Canvas

LIONS

A European woman in Kenya was walking along a dirt road near her home when she suddenly saw a lioness with cubs coming towards her. The woman, who was carrying one child and leading another by the hand, froze on the spot. Lionesses are extremely nervous and usually very aggressive when with cubs. The lioness moved towards the terrified woman, stopping just short of her, and smelled her small child. She stared at the poor woman for what must have seemed an eternity. The lioness then turned around, went back and collected her cubs, and disappeared into the bush. The very shaken mother returned home without ever being touched. The year was 1960. What made the lioness so lenient?

About two years earlier, seven Novambo tribesmen were walking home in the Etosha Pan of Namibia (Southwest Africa at that time). This is a very open area. They came upon a pride of lions that were acting very aggressive towards them. So threatened, they immediately climbed a stunted tree trunk as high as they could and waited...and waited. Midday turned to afternoon. Afternoon turned to evening. By then the lions had gathered underneath them, showing more and more interest in getting at the trembling men. At dusk, one lion leaped up and clawed one of the men right out of the tree.

All of the lions were on the poor man before he even hit the ground. The six remaining men in the tree could see their comrade being torn to pieces while hearing his very brief, hopeless cries, and the lions' grisly sounds that caused them. They now realized what the lions already knew: There was a good supply of food trapped on that tree trunk above the lions. All they had to do was leap up and pluck that food into their laps. Tragically for the remaining men, that is just what happened, as one by one they were pulled out of the tree into the midst of the waiting lions, to be eaten alive. When park rangers came upon the terrible scene the next day they saw the lions sitting under that stunted tree, all with full bellies. Above them, clinging for his life was one last man — one very demented survivor.

The great South African conservationist, Ian Player, told this true story to me. In the early 1980s, he and hunter Orlando Celluci were game-viewing with park ranger John Dixon when they came upon three menacing lions that showed no fear of them. They escaped unharmed but learned later that Novambo tribespeople in the area believe that those lions were descendants of earlier man-eaters.

The Citizen

April 2, 1990

HIT LION ON HEAD — SAVED PAL

VICTORIA FALLS — An elderly man sustained injuries and was admitted to hospital at Victoria Falls at the week-end after being mauled by a lion. National park officials said the man had been herding cattle with a friend, 26 km south-west of this tourist resort town when the lion suddenly attacked him, Ziana news agency reports. His friend saved him from being fatally mauled by hitting the lion on the head with a rod until the beast ran off into the bush. The attack was reported to the police and the injured man was taken to hospital where his condition is reported to be stable. — Sapa.

Distraction, Oil on Canvas

THE LION IN HISTORY

Of all the wild animals on earth, the lion, more than any other animal, has created the greatest impression on man. It is the "King of Beasts," a symbol of strength, majesty, bravery, and ferocity. Nations have adopted the lion as their national emblem. It appears on the coat of arms of cities, towns, and families. Lions served as mascots for kings. The lion appears among the earliest drawings made by humans and is still used today as a symbol for countries and corporations. They were and are used as entertainers, from ancient Roman to modern circuses. They have been painted and sculpted as works of fine art as well as used in present-day advertising. Egyptian and Assyrian sphinxes had the body of a lion. The great Sphinx itself is a monumental statement by a pharaoh who wanted to be remembered as a lion. Our legends and folklore are filled with stories of lions.

Lions have played a very bloody part in history. They were even used in war, although more for their dramatic effect than for any actual military value. Ramses II went into battle in a chariot flanked by his special lion, Auto-m-nekht, which very effectively kept people away from him. Marc Antony is supposed to have driven a chariot pulled by lions. The Assyrians and Babylonians used lions as bodyguards and to eat prisoners — a popular form of entertainment except, of course, for the prisoners.

Although the use of lions in war was neither widespread nor particularly successful, the same cannot be said of lions used for executions and in the Roman arena. No fewer than fifty thousand lions are recorded as having been sent to the Coliseum between 80 and 120 A.D. Pompeii had six hundred in its coliseum during one festive period alone. In 185 B.C., Marcus Fuvius Nobilior ordered that all lions and leopards captured by Romans were to be killed in arena events. Julius Caesar celebrated the consecration of the Forum in Rome by having four hundred lions slaughtered by various means, mainly by men.

The stories of Christians being thrown to lions are well documented. It was Nero who began the practice. A fire destroyed half of Rome and he blamed the Christians. In an orgy of blood lust, he had Christian prisoners dressed in animal skins and put into the arena, where they were killed and eaten by lions. Gladiators, too, were killed in large numbers by the lions, which were invariably starved into a state of frenzy before the contests. Some gladiators wore a gauntlet, carried a shield, and used a spear, or occasionally a sword or trident. Some faced the lions while armed only with a net or cloak, with which they were supposed to confuse and then strangle the lion. These desperate men were recruited from the ranks of criminals, prisoners of war, or young men in need of money. They were well trained and many apparently took pride in their status. Some fought lions with such courage that, if they were criminals or prisoners, and if they survived, they were freed. Once Nero had his mounted guards, armed with lances, fight three hundred lions in the arena.

From the time they were introduced into the arena (around 270 B.C.), until man-versus-animal events were abolished some five hundred years later, thousands of gladiators and helpless prisoners were killed and occasionally eaten by lions in front of fascinated audiences. And if the humans could be counted in the thousands, the lions that were killed could be counted in the tens of thousands. It was the huge toll of lions killed in the arena that made them extinct in Rome and the surrounding region. Lion hunting in biblical days must have been costly in terms of lives: Tiglathpileser is said to have killed more than a hundred lions on foot, and more than seven hundred from his chariot. Assurnasirpal is reputed to have killed more than three hundred lions with a spear. The Greeks in Homer's time hunted lions with abandon and, according to Homer, man-eating lions, which probably escaped or were still in outlying areas, presented a serious problem for the citizens. Can you imagine being the famous Marathon runner, knowing that he faced such an additional hurdle?

The lion, common all over Africa and parts of Asia in early times, was also found in Europe and North America during the Pleistocene era. The older cave lions were 25 percent larger than modern lions or tigers. These larger ancestors, *Panthera atrox*, survived in North America as recently as ten thousand years ago, a time when they would have roamed the earth with man. The ice age and other climatic changes of the Pleistocene killed off the lion in North America and most of Europe. The distribution of lions in Africa is still very wide. Their ability to live without water in the desert, if there is enough prey, eliminates many natural barriers from blocking their spread into new territories. Very few other predators can survive crossing Africa's great deserts to find new hunting grounds.

The lion's extinction in the late nineteenth century in southernmost Africa and most of India was the result of relentless hunting by humans. The Barbary lion in northern Africa probably lasted until the desert war of 1941–42. The present-day decline in both India and Africa is also due to human pressure. The population explosion, which spreads human habitat into previously wild areas, increases man-lion conflicts in which the lion eventually loses. In India, severe over-grazing by livestock in the lions' last remaining refuge deprives its traditional wild prey of food and cover. These areas become deserts, reducing the wild game even more. The

The Pretoria News
March 28, 1989
MELBOURNE — A man was killed by lions in Melbourne Zoo and a girl was attacked by a tiger at Dubbo Zoo in separate incidents at the weekend. Police believe the man tried to confront the lions Tarzan-style to prove his martial arts prowess. When found, with the lower part of his body eaten, he was wearing kung fu pants and a black belt. His hands were clenched with lions' hair.

lions have only the encroaching cattle on which to feed. Even the people are competing for the lions' kills, driving away the lions so they can eat or sell the meat and hides. However, after reading a draft of this book, George Schaller, the great field scientist and Director of Science for Wildlife Conservation International at the Wildlife Conservation Society in New York, told me that there is now a core area in India with little livestock and much wildlife for the lions to prey upon. Says he, "Things have improved greatly in the past quarter century."

The history of lions and man cannot be accurately recorded without noting that there is a lot of killing — and on both sides. Up until recent times lions have been considered vermin. They are certainly not vermin to the television viewer sitting comfortably in a big city, but to an African native, living a barely sustainable existence, lions are a very real problem. They have eaten his ancestors and probably some recent relatives and he does not want them walking outside his hut every night. I believe that the killing of lions started out as self-defense. It probably progressed to the protection of livestock, then to the proving of manhood, and today to the sport of hunting.

The death of people caused by African man-eaters of any type is not something that makes the front pages. Very little such news reaches the outside world. Small wonder, I suppose, since tourism, an important source of revenue in most African countries, would be adversely affected. If you talk with these countries' chambers of commerce or their travel agents, you would think no tourist ever gets hurt. I am certainly not trying to be an alarmist. I do believe that statistically these occurrences are very rare. They do, however, happen — and they happen more than we realize. All the big cats are opportunists and they just don't turn down any easy meal. Unlike many biologists, I believe most lions are capable of being man-eaters under the right circumstances.

Hunting by Man

The issue of hunting lions or any other animal is a controversial topic these days. It seems to me that each side has little understanding for the other's point of view. I have great respect for those who do not think we should kill animals. I do not understand, however, the convenient thought process that allows some, so inclined, to be blind to the fact that we let others do that killing for us. If we eat meat or fish, or wear leather belts, shoes, coats, or furs, we are subsidizing the killing of animals. Is this convenient hypocrisy on our part?

I also respect those who love the sport of hunting, which is truly so crucial in effectively preserving our wildlife. Hunting is directly responsible for the preservation of many species. Hunting licenses in the United States provide more conservation funds to their states than the combined donations of the Nature Conservancy, National Wildlife Federation, and the National Audubon Society. The wild turkey in the United States would be extinct were it not for hunter conservation programs. The turkey now exists in every state in the union except Alaska.

The work done by the scientific community, particularly field biologists, cannot be underestimated. It is awesome. However, that information would be incomplete without the mountains of data provided by the hunting fraternity. The lion and other game animals would be extinct in many places were it not for the conservation programs and the currency that hunting provides. These are effective incentives for local villages to preserve many species. If we are to really know this wonderful animal called the lion, all of these perspectives are necessary. Too many anti-hunters have no idea how cruel their position often is to the hunted animal. Most animals, especially in Africa, meet death by being eaten alive, including the lordly lion. I do not know about others, but I would much rather be shot than eaten alive by wild animals. Both viewpoints have their share of lunatics, but they also have some common goals that I think we should all work on together.

Vital Statistics

The African lion's scientific name is *Panthera leo*. There is an isolated remnant race in the Gir Forest of India. Its technical name is the same but I'm sure the taxonomists will change that. Leo, a favorite nickname for the lion, is a derivative of the Greek word *leon*, for lion.

Range

The lion is found today throughout much of sub-Saharan Africa. Between one hundred and two hundred lions live in the Gir Forest Sanctuary in Gujarat Pradesh, India. Some scientists say the Indian lion has a scantier mane, longer elbow and tail tufts, and fuller belly fringe with relatively shorter, heavier legs for its length of body, than the African lion.

As an artist, the only difference I have noticed is that the Indian lion seems to have a flatter head than its African cousin. I helped raise money to purchase a pair of Asiatic lions for the Knoxville Zoo in the late 1970s when Guy Smith was its director.

My studies of these two lions, as well as others, led to that conclusion. However, there may very well be something unrelated to the bone structure such as muscle form or even the ears in relation to the forehead that communicates the difference that I see. Taxonomists spend a great deal of time measuring skulls and, since they don't mention anything about differences in skull measurements in their conclusions, you should take my observation as that of an imaginative artist and not a scientist. But you can also ask a mother how she can tell which one of her children is coming down the stairs by sound alone when no one else can. However, these lions seem to be very much like their African cousins in most other respects.

SIZE

Panthera leo is the second largest and longest member of the family of Felidae. An average lion weighs between 270 and 440 pounds and is seven and a half to ten feet in length. Males are about 30 percent larger than females. A lion can, in exceptional cases, weigh up to a quarter of a ton (533 pounds, observed by biologist Austin Roberts). It can measure over ten feet from nose to tail tip, and tower seven feet when it rises up at the end of a charge. According to C. Guggisberg in his book Simba, "it has the strength of ten men and has been seen to clear a twelve-foot wide chasm when driven by desperation."

Tony Dyer heard of lions measuring ten feet, six inches from the tip of the nose to the last joint of the tail. However, he has seen no such lion in East Africa. Both Donald Ker and Syd Downey, partners in the famous safari firm of Ker & Downey, say the largest lions they have ever seen or had record of measured nine feet, seven inches. Ker says the very largest lions stand about three feet, six inches at the shoulder and weigh five hundred pounds. Delia and Mark Owens describe one of their lions, "Satan," as a very big male lion at twelve feet, four inches long and more than four feet tall. That is one huge lion. By contrast, the weights of the largest Indian tigers approach six hundred pounds.

LIFESPAN

As with humans, the females live longer than males. Although a lion may live about twenty years in captivity, in the wild, with the harsher life it must lead, a male is lucky to live nine to twelve years and a female thirteen to seventeen because of her constant protection by the pride. At ten, a lioness is still in her peak breeding years. Serengeti females can live as long as eighteen years and normally remain fertile until they are about fifteen. A lion will live in grasslands, dry forests, woodlands, savannas, and deserts. For food it preys upon wildebeest, zebra, buffalo, and any reasonably sized antelope in its territory. When times are hard they will eat anything they can catch.

LIFESTYLES

Generally lions live in prides. A lion pride is a group of adult females with dependent young, and a group of transient males. The pride territory is where the female group of mothers, daughters, grandmothers, and cubs lives for generations. Males come into the pride as a group, taking it over by driving out the incumbent males. They father cubs and defend the pride against other marauding bands of nomadic males. Every few years the resident male coalition is replaced by yet another group. This is another example of nature's way of maintaining the species by limiting inbreeding. There will be more on this in the population section.

Lions are not considered good tree climbers but they can and will use trees to scan the local landscape for prey and will sometimes climb them to escape buffalo and hyenas. I used to see lions in the Lake Manyara National Park in Tanzania climb trees far more often than they do now. In his book The Serengeti Lion George Schaller says this behavior represents a habit that may have been initiated by a prolonged fly epidemic, and has since been transmitted culturally. Most lion tree-climbing is done on easy-to-climb slanted limbs, but they are capable of climbing vertical, limbless trees as well. Lion trainer Josip Marcan of Deland, Florida, says that although a big male may find it difficult, it is not much

Awareness, Oil on Canvas

for a lioness to climb his palm trees, especially smaller ones. *The Johannesburg Star* editor James Clark described a lioness climbing a vertical telephone pole up to forty feet to get at meat.

Adult lions are extremely tolerant of the sun and will frequently spend the whole day in the open, even though shade is available within easy walking distance. On other days they might just as soon move into a kopje (rock pile) or lie beneath a tree. They certainly can relax! In Amboseli I saw a very pretty, honey-colored male sleeping with his legs in the air. He got up to stretch and his yawn was so wide I wanted to yawn, too. He walked to another spot and flopped himself on the ground so hard that he gave a loud grunt, probably from knocking the wind out of himself.

As I noted before, desert lions can live for months on end without water. They obtain liquids from their prey and the few moist plants they eat. In their book *Cry of the Kalahari,* Delia and Mark Owens describe a lion, "Blue," which had not had a drink of water

in ten months. Her diet of springhare, mice, honey badgers, and bat-eared foxes was her only source of liquid. She often had to walk ten miles at night to find food. The Owenses also told me of giraffe, springbok, gemsbok, and hartebeest that could live almost indefinitely without water. They got moisture only from the vegetation they ate.

Lions don't often rest in water on hot days. They are not considered good swimmers, even though I have witnessed them wading and swimming in the Chobe River and its tributaries in Botswana. I did not find this strange, as most of their prey lives on islands in the wet season. Lions that are not afraid of water have a lot more food available.

Ticks infest most lions, especially around the ears, neck, and groin. I have never seen a lion without ticks. One day, while waiting for the pride to move, I counted over 120 visible ticks on one lioness on just the one side visible to me.

Lions have great recuperative power and even large wounds tend to heal completely. Schaller describes a male lion that was bitten through the nasal bones, and was fully recovered within six weeks. I found an injured lion at dusk in Botswana. It was on its last legs and surrounded by menacing hyenas. It had a very old scar on its neck where the skin had been torn off. About a dozen square inches of flesh had been exposed and had dried in that condition. The wound was at least a few months old. I thought it amazing that it had survived so long considering how deadly infections can be in Africa.

Victoria Falls African Crowned Eagle, Oil on Canvas

The Sunday Times
December 6, 1992

PANICKY TOURISTS TAKE ANGRY LION FOR A RIDE

Wealthy Arab businessmen had a narrow escape with a lion in a local game park…some of SA's wildlife. But things took a terrifying turn when a male lion sauntered over to their car and nonchalantly swatted at Nazerian's window. Nazerian said: "He punched at the window, knocking the mirror. It was as if he was trying to get me." He swerved at the lion, and then drove off as fast as he could. But this particular lion was not going to be brushed off. "In my rear mirror, I saw him running behind us. Then he landed with his belly on the boot, claws on the roof, and his legs dragging on the ground. I swung the car from side to side. He clung on for about two minutes, all the while swiping at the head of one of the board members. Eventually he was shaken off, and roared with anger." Ellen Stack, who has worked for the park for 24 years, said: "The lions are very playful, especially when it has been raining. Maybe the lion mistook the car for the van which brings their food. They often climb all over it and chase it because they know it." Nazerian and his guests took a less optimistic view of the affair. Hardly surprising, considering that the car in which they were driving was a Lancia, with a canvas roof.

SENSES

Like most cats, lions see better at night because of the extra light that bounces to their retina from a special reflecting layer, the *Tapetum lucidum*. This increases their sensitivity even to starlight. At night they really do seem like kings, afraid of nothing, much less concerned about being seen by either humans or their prey. Their night vision is much better than most other animals, and they know it. A brave young Masai moran warrior, who thinks nothing of charging into a pride of lions in daylight, will be terrified of any lion at night. J.A. Hunter, while in a boma blind at night with his Masai tracker, describes how the poor man's attitude changed drastically in the dark. "To my astonishment, I heard him whisper *'Taballo!'* Masai for 'Wait!' I glanced over at him and saw the man was paralyzed with fear. The unfamiliar experience of seeing lions at night from a boma had completely unnerved him, yet in daylight this man would walk up to an infuriated lion with nothing but his spear."

An alert lion has its ears cocked, its eyes wide-open, staring intently at whatever has its attention, and is sometimes flicking its tail. Other lions seeing this will respond to the gesture by becom-

ing alert also, not unlike one hunting dog backing another on point. At night, lions are almost a different species. Darkness is their element. Incredibly acute hearing augments their excellent eyesight.

In his book *Into Africa*, Craig Packer describes a lioness that started to panic while on a half-eaten zebra, not in fear of the hyenas that were present, but of whatever larger danger the hyenas' calls might attract. The lioness had strayed into another pride's territory. Alerted by something, she fled onto a nearby kopje. Just moments later, a large male lion charged up and scattered the hyenas from the remains. The lioness must have heard him coming from nearly a mile away.

In the Okavango in 1996, I witnessed a lioness moving in our direction, completely ignoring and passing a reasonably closely warthog. She traveled on a straight route for what our vehicle later measured as one and a third miles. She walked quickly and directly through two open fields and three thickly wooded sections to where three cheetahs had just killed a young wildebeest. At the sight of the lioness the cheetahs were gone in a flash. That lioness had to have heard the kill from that distance. The little wind present was a very slight cross wind and it would have been impossible for her to see through all the vegetation. I can only credit this to an extraordinary sense of hearing. My tracker driver thought it quite normal.

Movie photographer Mike Penman of Botswana disagrees with Schaller's opinion that lions cannot distinguish color. While making the film *Eternal Enemies,* he said the lions that they were working with eventually accepted the photographer Joubert's red car, yet they would never accept any other cars of the same make and model, the only difference being that of the red color. However, this might be explained by something else, since it was hardly tested for other theories. Retired professional hunter and conservationist Tony Dyer is of the opinion that on very dark nights, lions do little or no killing. Even their remarkable eyesight is affected.

SCENT

One way lions communicate is through olfaction, scent-marking, and smelling. Spraying and scraping are used to lay claim to an area, a lioness in heat, a kill, or anything else Leo wants to claim. Scent functions as a spacing mechanism, letting other lions know what they may be up against should they go any farther.

When a male, or males, takes over a new territory by driving out the resident males, the new males scent-mark frequently and roar at short intervals. Males rarely pass a marking spot without giving it a squirt or two. Females also mark bushes, but not as persistently as do males.

A scrape mark is another type of olfactory and visual signpost used by male and female lions. The sign is made when the individual hunches its back, lowers its rump, and rakes its back feet over the ground, tearing up the turf with its claws while dribbling urine into the soil.

Packer found that a male frequently rubs the bushes with his head prior to marking. The odors may help create a characteristic pride odor, as they are transferred by the head-rubbing with which lions regularly greet each other. Every lion leaves tracks, urine, and feces in its environment; these also serve as signals to other lions passing by later. Lions of all ages sharpen the claws of their forepaws by raking them down the trunks of trees, which is yet another form of marking a territory.

As well as marking territory, scent identifies the individual lion that left the mark, and its intensity indicates how long ago it passed the spot. It also communicates the condition of females in estrus. Schaller reported that Serengeti lions can locate each other with scent, and he observed one male following the trail of two others for a kilometer. Kalahari lions appear to be less successful at this, especially in the dry season, possibly because scent deteriorates more rapidly in the arid desert heat. Unlike most other writers, Schaller insists that lions also have a superior sense of smell, having seen them sniffing at a zigzagging trail for over a mile to find their way.

Norman Carr had no small amount of experience with lions. While doing research on lions in Northern Rhodesia (now Zambia), he raised a pair of lions with the game park's permission from 1957

Chobe Elephant, Oil on Canvas

to 1961. He said they consistently used wind to their advantage when hunting. "It was noticeable that they were always conscious of the wind; any supporting flanking movement was invariably made from down-wind. The longer one lives among wild animals the more one realizes what an important part scent, and the wind which wafts it, play in the lives of all wild mammals whether they are the predators or the prey."

The Saturday Star
FOREIGN NEWS SERVICE
February 20, 1993
LION'S VICTIM PROUD OF ORDEAL

LONDON — A young man who was badly mauled by a male lion after climbing into its cage at London Zoo has been transferred from hospital to a psychiatric unit. The young man, Ben Silcock (27), a diagnosed schizophrenic, climbed into the lion's enclosure seven weeks ago to protest against the caging of the big cats.

COMMUNICATION

Lions and other big cats have very expressive facial movements and are successful at making their feelings known not only to other lions but to humans as well. As an artist I am sure this trait is why I like them so much. Signals used at close range can be very complex. Teeth, lips, ears, tail, and other parts of the body convey ever-changing signal patterns. Schaller points to a study by Leyhausen that distinguished between aggressive threat and defensive threat in the facial expressions of the house cat. In aggressive threat the mouth is almost closed, the ears are erect and twisted so that their backs face forward, and the pupils of the eyes are small. In defensive threat the canines are exposed and the lips withdrawn, the ears are flattened, and the pupils are large. Lions do the same. Olfactory, visual markings, and of course their wonderful roaring, are used for long–distance communication. Lions apparently need and use these complex signals to regulate their family structure.

George Adamson states that lions are sensitive creatures and dislike being stared at. Their eyes can have a detached glare, which gives the impression the lion is looking through rather than at the observer. A snarling face with exposed teeth, although defensive in nature, is a warning that an attack may be imminent. These expressions are common at kills and typical of courting lions. In pursuit of prey, lions use the alert, but not snarling, expression. Schaller never saw a lion attack another that rolled submissively on its back. When a male rushes a lioness, he will stop if she has crouched and her head–twisted to the side. Young males placing their faces on the ground won't be harassed further when chased by an adult. This occurs only with pride members, however. When new males take over a pride they are ruthless to any other males or cubs in their new pride.

A "Flehmen" facial expression is seen when a lion lifts its head into the air, upper lips raised, teeth bared, tongue sticking out. These contortions enhance their sense of smell by passing odors over an area filled with sensory cells located in the roof of the mouth, called the vomeronasal organ. They are literally "tasting" the scent.

Another important method of communication between lions is touch. Aside from normal accidental rubbing and touching, lions also seek physical contact. Resting lions often initiate contact by head-rubbing, social licking, and other peaceful tactile gestures. These actions promote group cohesion and serve the same purpose as grooming does in primate societies. Head-rubbing occurs particularly after animals have been separated. Cubs run to their mother and rub against her after she returns from a hunt. Rubbing and licking function as a form of greeting. It is quite possible that each lion pride has a distinct group odor. This group odor would help to unite the group. Head-rubbing would tend to spread group odor among the members.

Lions often lick one another. After a meal, a group member will lick the throat of another lion. They probably lick one another's fur to get at parts of the body not easily reached. They lick each other mutually, which may help to dry an animal after a rain or being in water. Lionesses in particular seem to enjoy this and most other forms of social licking. Anal sniffing is common when a lioness is in estrus, or when lions appear to be uncertain about identities.

VOCALIZATION

By the age of one month, lion cubs emit, in rudimentary form, all the sounds that adults make, although the full roar is not displayed until adolescence. The lion possesses a ligament enabling expansion of the larynx for the increased resonance that results in the lion's exceptionally loud and awesome roar. The abdomen sucks in visibly and then expands when roaring. With his belly pushing into his gut, forcing the huge chest to heave out a sound so awesome and primitive, it seems as if the very ground beneath you vibrates. Roaring by any group member often stimulates others to join, and their powerful chorale is one of the great animal sounds in nature. Females, also roar, but their voices are neither as deep nor as loud as the male.

Lions roar mostly at night when it is cooler and damper than during the day. The warm daylight air is less dense and not as good a conductor of sound. Roaring is not easy, and lions don't like to strain themselves in the heat of the day. They roar mostly in calm weather. They don't waste energy roaring when it is too windy for their calls to be carried into the night. On still nights you can hear a lion roar from five miles away. On a clear, cold, African night, sounds travel well, and three miles is not at all too great a range to hear them roar. British Army Colonel

Stevenson-Hamilton said it is possible under ideal conditions to hear them for up to six miles. And Mark and Delia Owens in *Cry of the Kalahari* write, "In the valley, and under the conditions described, the sound carries the farthest, up to eight miles, to our comparatively unspecialized human ear."

Lions roar most during seasons of plentiful prey, when nomads or neighbors might be tempted to raid their area. Roaring tells the strangers how many lions occupy a given territory and where they are at the moment. Roaring also tells companions what is happening within the pride. Lions usually roar while standing.

To me a lion's roaring, especially at night is pure magic. When you are in a tent and close to the ground, and you can hear that deep, thundering bellow, all your perceptions are heightened, and in my case, the sound is imprinted forever in your mind. If the lion is close, and particularly if it is night, it is one hell of an experience. My artist's imagination gives me license to tell you that it sounds like it emanates from the very bowels of the earth. If a pride is scattered and you are camped in the middle of them, I can promise you a night you shall not soon forget. Hearing a lion's roar is one of my favorite aspects of the delicious African night.

I am thrilled by the trumpet blast of an elephant, and the deep, bellowing grunting of a hippo, but the roar of a lion is the "big enchilada." It is just breathtaking. While on safari with our friends Dale and Mary Hudson we had lions roaring within feet of us. They were roaring back and forth while walking as our vehicle kept pace with them. Mary says it was one of the most exciting things she has ever witnessed.

Thomas S. Arbuthnot, former Dean of the University of Pittsburgh Medical School, describes vividly the roar in his book *African Hunt*. After a very upset lion came close to him he

> took a deep breath and relaxed. I pondered
> over a man's five senses; they can attune
> themselves to a high pitch over lions in the
> grass; they can activate themselves to the
> nth degree, but they register only accelera-

tion—not judgment. The lion was fury incarnate. I never knew that any animal could work itself into such a state. Its eyes fairly blazed; every hair on its body stood on end. Through its partly open mouth poured a continuous volume of deep-toned, rumbling growls that swelled to a roar. Its long, lashing tail stood high, practically at right angles to its back. His fury was a magnificent thing to see and hear. We use the term "blood curdling." There can, of course, be no congealing of the blood, but it is easy to imagine that a roar such as we heard, together with the sudden appearance of the massive head, could distinctly upset a weaker animal's calculations and make it fairly easy prey.

Not all lions however are so noisy. Tony Dyer tells of lions preying on the cattle of the Orma tribesmen in Kenya that have become silent. This is because these gentle people who have lived with cattle and lions for more than two thousand years persistently hunt lions when they hear them or see tracks near their cattle. Lions and the Orma still share the same country, but the lions have evolved into a very quiet animal that does not roar near the Orma's camps.

Lions spend most of their time doing absolutely nothing. In his research on lions, Craig Packer very cleverly used these many frustrating hours of dullness to his advantage. He used the lions' recorded roars to conjure up "cooperation on demand." He put a strange lion's roar on the speakers and noted all types of reactions. "Whenever we played the recorded roar of a nomadic male to a group of resident males, the residents instantly became alert, listening intently. Once the recording ended, they would quickly rise and walk determinedly toward the speaker, ready to evict the invader. On they came, continuing right past the speaker, within a few feet of the car, heading off in the direction where the stranger must be."

Roaring ranges from barely perceptible grunts to full roars. Although the sounds differ in loudness, duration, and frequency of emission, all are of a low frequency. Soft roaring is used as a

The Pretoria News
January 24, 1995
LODGE FINED AFTER WOMAN KILLED BY LIONS
DURBAN — Zululand's Phinda Lodge was fined R 20,000 by a magistrate here yesterday in connection with the death of a woman who was mauled by lions at the lodge last year, it was reported. The chairman of Phinda's board of directors, David Boyd Varty, pleaded guilty to culpable homicide in the Durban Magistrate's Court. In a statement, Mr. Vary admitted the lodge had been negligent and had caused the death of Grace Ann Strous. Mrs. Strous was mauled to death by three lions on April 22.

contact call, letting others know of the lion's whereabouts. Loud roaring, the lion's best-known vocalization, is usually used where they are not harassed.

Safari and hunting guide Robin Hurt, in a letter to me, says this about the lion's roar:

If you spend enough time in the African bush, on safari, sooner or later you will have lion come into your camp at night. A lion roaring at close proximity to someone trying to sleep in a safari cot can be an intimidating experience, whether for a rank amateur or a seasoned hunter! The volume of a lion's roar is such that it can easily be heard up to five miles away. Close up, it makes the hair on the back of your neck stand up. It immediately gets your full attention, like nothing else can!

Resident lions may ignore roars they hear, but when searching for group members, they will respond immediately. The full roar, like the soft roar, advertises the animal's presence. It lets its group know its location. The roar also helps lions avoid contact with a trespasser, warning it of the consequences of proceeding any further. Although wolf-howls can distinguish individuals on the basis of any one howl, after experimenting with taped calls of Senora lions, Schaller thinks the cats lack that ability.

Whether or not pride-mates are successful at locating each other by roaring depends on whether the recipient of the call chooses to answer. At times, for instance, when on one of their kills, pride lionesses may not answer males. Since lionesses are the hunters, it is probably because they don't want the males taking over their kill.

Another form of vocalization, the *aaouu* sound can be tossed softly back and forth among them as they move through cover. It apparently helps the lions keep track of each other, as well as providing mutual reassurance. Growls vary considerably. Continuous, rolling growls are emitted by lions trying to avoid close contact, or responding to the growl of another animal even if that animal is obscured by vegetation. They are warnings to any unwanted intruder. To any animal, but certainly to a man on foot, the growl of a hidden lion is a very effective way of getting attention. Coughing is an explosive growl emitted once or twice in succession. It is similar to the growl but is a more

The Natal Witness
November 3, 1993
LIONS KILL TWO TAIWANESE STUDENTS
JOHANNESBURG — Two young Taiwanese died after being mauled by Kalahari lions at the Honeydew Lion Park. They were attacked by the pride of 11 lions as they posed for photographs two metres from the beasts. Their three friends escaped unharmed. Warning notices are posted throughout the park and on the back of the entry tickets. Game warden Eric Meyer said he was alerted about the attack shortly after 10 am when three young Chinese sped up in their car, hooting, screaming and gesticulating. He rushed to the spot where the pride of 11 lions had been sleeping under trees and saw some of the five-year-old lionesses shaking the couple by their necks.

The Pretoria News
June 20, 1996
LONE GOLFER
A Johannesburg stockbroker tells of a visiting American banker who played a round of golf at Victoria Falls' Elephant Hills course. At the conclusion of 18 holes, during which he encountered no other golfers, he was met by a crowd of about two dozen spectators who applauded him as he putted out the final green. Bemused, he asked: "Why the accolades? Why the spectators?" "Didn't you see the sign on the first tee? It discouraged golf today because a lioness and her cubs were prowling the course." The banker continues to dine out on the story.

intimidating threat. They also make grunting sounds, which remind me of the sounds of someone very constipated. Males also meow during copulation.

Sometimes at night, after our mopane fire had died down and the whole camp was asleep, a serenade of lions roaring in the distance would keep me very alert. No matter how far off they might be, this sound always creates great excitement in any camp. It is a disappointment on the nights that I do not hear them.

COLORATION

Adult lion coloration ranges from gray to yellow-tan, with the male's mane ranging from honey–yellow to cinnamon or black. Cubs have a coat not unlike soft steel wool, with dark brown spots on a light tawny background. Kenyan conservationist Tony Dyer says there is a phase of lions in the Melawa Valley that not only have spots that remain on their coat into maturity but which may be very pronounced, as in the king cheetah. Unfortunately, we have little information about them.

MANE

A male lion's mane is the very long hair that grows behind the face and all around the neck, and which can reach back beyond the shoulders and actually run the length of the belly. But belly hair is much less frequent in wild males. The size and extent of the mane and its color vary widely between individuals. It also varies with age. Its presence in an adult male lion adds to his apparent size, which certainly has an intimidating effect on his enemies. The mane is frequently darker than the tawny color of the rest of the body. Around the face there is a lighter fringe of long hairs. A male normally begins to show some mane development around a year old, but this is relatively insignificant until between three and four years of age. At that time, males grow very quickly in both overall body size and mane length. These changes indicate that the big cat has reached sexual maturity.

Some adult males never develop manes. The man-eaters of Tsavo were huge animals with practically no manes at all. Male lions may also have long tufts of hair on each elbow. The extent

of this tuft is relative to the degree of development of the mane. Lions in captivity have larger manes, probably because of the lack of wear and tear that would be experienced in the bush. N. Hollister compared young captive lions in the area around Nairobi with wild adults killed in the same area. He found that captivity results in darker pelages (gray or tan coloration, where in the wild those particular areas might be almost white); longer, darker, thicker mane and elbow tufts; and a greater area of mane over the top of the shoulders and along the belly. Very small manes can occur in females, although this is rare. According to Guggisberg, in his book *Simba*, castration prevents development or causes the loss of the mane in adult males. Professional hunter Fred Bartlett says that male coastal lions usually have no mane, or occasionally only a short ridge along the neck, and that it is difficult to tell the difference between the sexes. It is generally agreed that the biggest manes are grown by lions in cool, fairly open country.

Thomas Gnoske, a zoologist from the Field Museum in Chicago, and Dr. Kerbis Peterhans of Roosevelt University in Chicago have recently (2001) done some very convincing studies declaring that under normal circumstances lions grow longer manes if they live in higher altitudes and that manes are a function of elevation and climate. Very old males usually have less mane. In pride life, the mane has clear functions and advantages. The male's mane increases his apparent size and makes him look more impressive when courting. It's theorized that the size of the mane must also warn adversaries of the male's power. The mane also distinguishes two lions from great distances. Experimenting with dummy lions, Packer found that females preferred males with longer and darker manes. Both sexes take great pains to guard their areas from intrusions of their own gender, but sometimes they will accept outsiders of the opposite sex. Therefore it would be advantageous for a male to be recognized as a male from a distance, and thus be able to go towards a lioness with much less fear of attack. The mane also allows males to recognize each other long before any combat starts.

Gentle Breeze, Oil on Canvas

The Pretoria News
June 17, 1988

HARARE — A 29-year old Harare woman was admitted to hospital today after being attacked by a lioness at Mana Pools holiday resort [on the Zambezi River]. Ms. Smith was on a canoeing trip when she was attacked by the lioness while in a sleeping bag in the open. Ms. Smith said she was waiting for specialists to determine her condition. "I am still in shock, I have been given morphine and really cannot say much."

Helen's Lions, Oil on Canvas

Bachelor Evening, Oil on Canvas

TAIL

At the tip of the tail of both males and females is a tuft of long, dark hairs, forming a black tassel. Schaller suggests that occasionally flicking this tuft may help the cubs or male keep a lioness in sight when traveling. At the tip of the tail in this tuft is usually a spur or horny point. It is fairly small and is not attached to the vertebral column. Its purpose is not known.

PELAGE

The gray-blue eyes of the cubs turn into the amber color of adults' eyes between two and three months old. A cub's fur is soft and woolly, a grayish-yellow or pale brown color, and variously marked with spots or stripes. This pattern varies considerably among individual cubs. The spots are frequently darkest and most numerous on the forehead. Biologist J. Pocock describes a heavily spotted cub, in which the spots on the back and flanks form rosettes fused into transverse chains, forming a striped effect. At the other extreme, in *Simba*, Guggisberg reported a completely unmarked litter. At about three months, the coat starts to change; at about five months it is like an adult's. Around this time the tail tuft develops. By six months, some males may show a throat ruff.

Melanistic (black) lions are extremely rare. Albino lions are much more common, as is a white mutation that differs from a true albino by the normal yellow color that still appears in the mutant's eyes. Frederick Courteney Selous, one of the greatest African big game hunters, wrote that he observed both light- and dark-colored lions in the same brood. All lions that I have personally handled, both adults and cubs, have a distinct oily-greasy, lanolin-like feel to their coats. Considering the pelting a lion's coat takes in the rainy season, having a water repellant hide does not surprise me at all. It is strange, however, that it does not seem to show up in the literature that I've read on lion pelage.

The Johannesburg Star
February 11, 1985
LION NIPPED OFF THREE FINGERS
NAIROBI — A man lost three fingers when he stuck his arm into a cage at an agricultural fair to pat a lion on display, it was reported here yesterday. "Quick action by prison wardens separated the man from the lion's jaws, minus his fingers," the report said. — Sapa-Associated Press.

AGE

Cubs' eyes are closed for the first week or so. Young cubs don't start learning to walk until their eyes are open and they can see. The lioness, however, keeps the cubs hidden for about another month, although she may move them from time to time. At about a month and a half, they will meet with the rest of the pride and at about two months of age will be able to keep up with the pride walking. Around this time, they also begin eating meat. Permanent incisor teeth replace milk teeth in under a year, with permanent canines appearing a month or two later. At the end of two years, the growth of the permanent teeth is complete. At this age they have a comically bowlegged look when viewed from the front.

At four months, a cub's shoulders are about half the height of its mother's. At a year its shoulders are 75 to 80 percent of an adult female's. At two years the male's shoulder height will already be that of the adult lioness and he will start showing his mane. At three to four years, females will look the same as the other adult lionesses from a distance. In addition to being larger, males can be distinguished by their still incompletely grown manes. At five years, there is very little difference between young lions and their parents. As I said earlier, most lions live for ten to fifteen years, but some individuals survive into their twenties. I have always thought the lions in the Ngorongoro Crater were larger than most other lions, even those of the Kalahari. Packer and Schaller attribute the Ngorongoro Crater lions' size to their consistent supply of food throughout the year. They don't have the long periods of food scarcity found in other areas where principal prey animals are migratory. Much more complete growth information on lions can be found in the paper by Smuts, Anderson, and Austin, "Age Determination of the African Lion (*Panthera Leo*)."

The death of a lion is no easier than the death of its prey. We think of the lion as the king of beasts and being the predator that he is, many of us assume that a lion dies in its sleep at the end of a long life. In most cases the truth is quite different. Death is much like it is for their prey: They are eaten alive, usually by hyenas, wild dogs, leopards, or other lions. Death comes earliest to animals that are by themselves. One reason females live longer is the support of living in a pride. Nature is harsh and most African animals die a violent death. The lion is no exception, particularly untended cubs. Buffalo and elephant occasionally kill lion cubs when the opportunity arises. Buffalo also kill adult lions. After all, the buffalo may have a hell of a lot of meat to eat but that very meat contains the same muscle power the buffalo uses to toss not only his own weight around but the lion's weight as well. Hunting adults are often fatally kicked in the face by larger antelope. Porcupine quills in critical areas can incapacitate lions on occasion and crocodiles have pulled lions into the water, and not for swimming lessons. Many wounds that keep a lion from hunting cause it to starve. But they are usually eaten alive by hyenas or wild dogs before death by starvation occurs. Africans take only a small toll but that amount is greater as the population explodes. "Sport hunters" take very few but they take the prize specimens. However, they raise much money for these countries, prodding them to conserve places for lions as well as other animals for man to hunt (and photograph and just plain keep such places wild).

If a lion does reach advanced maturity, its choice of prey starts to diminish because of loss of teeth, or speed, or any other of the many losses in hunting ability that comes with the onset of old age. This process weakens the animal to the point where it cannot defend itself against other predators. The end of a pride male is almost always a sad and solitary affair. A thorn in the foot, or any leg injury which prevents him from stalking effectively, or an illness of any kind, even sheer exhaustion, and he is immediately at the mercy of the scavengers he once despised. A couple of hyenas can easily bring him down. Pride females may fare better, but eventually they, too, will be left to themselves to face these enemies.

African Crowned Cranes Victoria Falls, Oil on Canvas

The Pretoria News
August 13, 1997

FIVE LIONS WHICH KILLED 'ILLE-GALS' PUT DOWN

Kruger Park warden Harold Braack said: "It may appear cruel to a lot of people that we put down these lions, but we had no choice. Our experience with lions is that, once they have tasted human flesh, they don't stop. They turn into man-eaters and they never stop hunting for human beings."

FIVE KRUGER MAN-EATING LIONS KILLED

Five Kruger National Park lions which killed four Mozambicans attempting to enter South Africa illegally were put down on Monday, the National Parks Board said yesterday. Five of the illegal aliens on Sunday returned to the northern part of the Kruger Park, where they were attacked by the lions at the Kremetart drinking hole. Four climbed into a Mopane tree to escape the lions. A team, led by Kruger Park veterinarian Dr. Douw Grobler, tracked down the pride and destroyed the man-eating lions. A post mortem revealed human remains in the stomachs of all the lions. A purse with about R8 in Mozambican currency was found in the stomach of one of the animals. — Sapa.

LION'S STRENGTH

The lion's strength is legendary. An animal that looks like a pile of tawny-skinned jelly while at rest can instantly turn into steel muscle, teeth, and claws. Stories abound of their physical feats. Alfred Kleinsaw describes a zebra killed with one blow to the neck. With the lion out of the picture, an examination showed that the lion's blow had not even broken the skin on the zebra's neck, but that several square inches of the flesh beneath the skin was bruised. From that blow the zebra had died within a few seconds from a dislocated neck. African author and hunter Brian Herne told me of a lion named Blondie that casually loped over to a topi carcass and seized it by the throat, effortlessly lifting the 280-pound animal in his jaws and carrying it away.

Gustave Battenhausen relates an incident of a lion's power told to him by a ranch manager named Hans. Hans' wife joined the manager and a few others when they were tracking a wounded lioness right past her tent. Hans warned her it was a very dangerous business, and told her to stay well behind. Unfortunately, they walked right past the wounded lioness. She charged and Hans' wife, being last in line, was knocked down. Hans shot the lioness as it crouched on top of her. Then he pulled the lioness off and asked if she was all right. There wasn't a mark on her, not even a bruise, but she said that she felt very strange. Hans took her straight to the hospital, where they discovered that her liver had been completely smashed with one blow from the lioness. The woman died that night.

British Colonel John Henry Patterson, in his famous book, *The Man-Eaters Of Tsavo*, gives a vivid account of the strength of the lion:

The lion managed to get its head in below the canvas, seized him by the foot and pulled him out [of the tent]. *In desperation the unfortunate water-carrier clutched hold of a heavy box in a vain attempt to prevent himself being carried off, and dragged it with him until he was forced to let go by its being stopped by the side of the tent. He then caught hold of a tent rope, and clung tightly to it until it broke. As soon as the lion managed to get him clear of the tent, he sprang at his throat and after a few vicious shakes the poor* bhisti's *agonizing cries were silenced forever. The brute then seized him in his mouth, like a huge cat with a mouse, and ran up and down the* boma [thickets] *looking for a weak spot to break through. This he presently found and plunged into, dragging his victim with him and leaving shreds of torn cloth and flesh as ghastly evidence of his passage through the thorns.*

Unlike most man-eaters that carry their victims a good distance from the site of the kill, this lion showed complete disdain for fire and human shouts, and ate its meal in the light of the campfires, leaving only the skull, jaw, a few large bones, and two fingers.

You may hear that a lion is too big and heavy to climb trees,

Working Lady of The Evening, Oil on Canvas

especially vertically, but in the Serengeti I saw a lone lioness climb about thirty feet up an acacia tree to pinch a Thomson's gazelle from a leopard that had climbed higher to avoid the lioness. She brought the remains down from the tree and consumed it right under the leopard. Talk about rubbing it in. But I shudder to think how unsafe I'd be in any tree I would be able to climb. Lions are widely known to climb trees in Lake Manyara Park. In his autobiography, *From Sailor To Professional Hunter*, John Northcote says that while driving down the main road in the Queen Elizabeth Game Park, "Lion tails could be seen hanging down from the trees. They slept in the cool, keeping an eye on the huge herds of a thousand or more topi grazing nearby."

Bill Winter, another Kenyan Ker & Downey guide, describes this feat of lion strength. In the Narok district of Kenya, the Masai were having trouble with lions. Bill said a lion jumped through a substantial *boma*. These are thickets usually constructed with thornbrush and used as barriers on the ground to keep animals out. The lion killed a steer, and jumped back out of the *boma* with the steer in his mouth.

Having heard this story, and seen the barricade, I thought there was no way a lion could lift a 400-lb (181-kilo) steer and take it over a fence seven feet high and three feet wide and clear it. But when I actually went and saw the tracks, it was very evident where the kill had taken place inside the enclosure. It could be seen where the steer had been dragged to the edge, the lion's takeoff and outside where he had landed with it. I'd never have thought it possible, had I not seen it myself. Speaking to the Masai and asking them if they had experienced anything like it before, or heard of any incident like it, they said, "Yes". It wasn't usual but it did sometimes occur. What they thought happens is that the lion grasps the carcass, throws the weight of the cow or steer over its back and shoulder, much as one would carry a sack of

potatoes. Then it crouches and leaps over the fence, a feat of great strength and audacity.

J.A. Hunter describes the very same feat. It is so extraordinary that I left it out of this text until the feat was very reputably witnessed again.

COOPERATION

One critical attribute of a successful pride is cooperation. Lions cooperate in many ways that give them advantages over solitary cats. Their methods of hunting range from methodical planning to accidental success attributable to chance numerical superiority. More on that later. In their cooperation, while rearing their cubs for instance, one lioness, or even several members of the pride, may stay with all the cubs as baby-sitters while the rest of the lionesses hunt. In a pride, the non-hunting lionesses, cubs, and males generally share in kills unless the carcass is too small to feed the entire pride. In such a case the males, even if they did not participate in the hunt, frequently appropriate the entire kill, sometimes sharing it only with the cubs. Providing such security for the cubs while hunting food for the whole family has always been difficult for lionesses.

Lionesses will generally suckle other mothers' cubs, so that a cub can feed from three or four lionesses to get a full meal. If a lioness fails to produce enough milk or dies, her cubs are still able to stay in the pride and be raised by other females. The overall effect is that pride lionesses each rear to maturity two or more times the number of cubs that nomadic lionesses rear, even though both give birth as frequently, about a year or two apart. Although they each may give birth to two to four young it is very difficult for a single mother to raise them to maturity without the help of a pride. Since a young lion remains dependent for about two and a half years — a longer period of time than for any other species of cat — this cooperation enhances the individual lion's survival chances that much more. It enables the adults to teach a cub a larger repertoire of necessary skills, such as hunting in groups. Under the subject of cooperation, one just doesn't expect lions and hyenas to be mentioned in the same sentence, yet Tony Seth-Smith

The Pretoria News
June 7, 1988

ESCAPED CIRCUS LIONS KILL CHILDREN

RIO DE JANEIRO — Three lions broke through a wooden fence during a circus in southeastern Brazil and mauled to death two young children watching the performance. The accident happened during a Saturday performance of the Hungaro Circus in rural Colonel Fabriciano, 509 km northeast of Rio de Janiero. One lion grabbed Maira by the head, while a second mauled Marina, he said. Marina was killed instantly and Maira died on arrival at the hospital, according to Rio's do *Brasil* newspaper.

tells of a very interesting incident. Late one evening in the Mara, they saw a buffalo running away from three hyenas.

He was a big, old, bull buffalo and we were lucky enough to get so close to him that we suddenly realized that it wasn't three hyenas but two hyenas and a very young male lion, and the three of them proceeded to kill him as a team. The lion jumped on the buff's back first and then fell off underneath and grabbed it by the muzzle and the hyenas grabbed its back end and started pulling at its rear end and stomach. When the buffalo fell to the ground the lion got it by the throat and, among the three of them, they killed it. It was interesting to see a team operation by two quite different species. The young lion couldn't have killed the buffalo alone and we were interested to see whether they would all sit down and have a happy dinner party together. But the lion suddenly said: "Hey! Who are these hyenas hanging about here? I am a lion!" And he turned on the hyenas as much as to say: "Get off my buffalo." To our surprise the two hyenas then turned on the lion. The next minute the lion was on its back and we thought the two hyenas would kill it. He lashed out at them with all paws, snarling and growling, and then managed to leap out from underneath them and went off to lick his wounds behind a bush ten or fifteen yards away. After a little while, he came back again and, this time, fed on the buffalo, but on the other side of it, and he didn't attempt to be too proprietary about it.

TERRITORY

A pride's territory can range in size from about ten to more than one hundred square miles. These great differences are explained by the size and strength of the particular pride and the availability of prey. Nomads may follow their prey on migrations and range over a much larger area, although they do not defend it as a pride would. These nomads tend to have fairly amicable contacts and may share larger kills. There are very good reasons for them to get along with strangers. It is tough going for a loner and they can use a bit of help getting larger prey. Since they do not have to share that larger prey with a full pride, they can well afford to be generous with a lion whose help was necessary. By contrast, leopards, jaguars, and tigers survive in dense areas by their solitary habits, and by frequently settling for smaller prey.

Lions can live just about anywhere, including deserts, and most forests, as long as the area provides sufficient prey. Water is not that important except for their prey in arid areas. Animals such as oryx, kudu, and other smaller antelope get moisture from the desert plants. Lions are best suited to group-hunting larger prey in open areas. They get enough liquid from their kills. I have heard that lions living in the southwest Kalahari Desert sometimes eat tsama melons, which are known to have large amounts of water. The lions I saw on the Skeleton Coast of western Africa had no visible source of fresh water.

Lion pride areas can overlap, but direct confrontations are remarkably infrequent. Actual combat is rare because lions on the fringes of, or outside their areas, avoid members of other prides wherever possible. Land not claimed by a pride usually has a shortage of prey for much of the year. When most of the suitable land is already taken, new prides must crowd in between others, increasing the potential for conflict. Each pride confines itself to a definite area in which its members spend several years or, in the case of some lionesses, their whole life. The main requisites for the existence of a pride area are water sources for their prey and enough of that prey throughout the year. These conditions exist in the woodlands and along their edges but, for the most part, not on the plains. Most lions are not as adaptable as the lions of the

Last Ivory Hunter, Oil on Canvas

Kalahari Desert or the Skeleton Coast of western Africa. In Kenya's Nairobi Park, two lionesses with eight cubs remained in an area of thirty-four square kilometers, while their attending males wandered over an area more than four times that size. Pride areas seem to grow with the size of the pride as well as with the availability of prey. Desert lions see far less rain, and therefore less game, than do those in wetter areas like the Serengeti. These wetter areas have a greater number of large prey animals, and the resident lions are well fed.

Group territoriality is the preeminent cause of sociality in lions. If a female loses her territory, she usually loses all hope of raising cubs. If she is discovered in another pride's territory, she may well be killed. Once a pride contains fewer than three females, it will probably become extinct, being exterminated by its neighbors. A single lion's territory may include only a half-dozen barren kopjes *(rock out croppings)*, a few resident prey, and no permanent water supply. It is a territory that no pride would want.

All resident male coalitions are eventually defeated by younger and more vigorous challengers. No one stays on top forever. Solitary males may go for years before finally finding suitable male companions. Packer found that once they forge a partnership, these males are quite touching in their affection for each other.

They rub and pat each other, showing an attachment that they seldom display to females. It's true male bonding, I suppose, for once they have made the decision to team up, they are as close as brothers. You cannot determine the degree of genetic kinship from their behavior. Aside from the obvious, roaring and chasing away strangers is what a breeding male's responsibilities are all about. This is the reason pride males roam a larger area than the females.

Norman Carr suggests that nomad lions challenging pride males have an advantage in that they are tough and in good condition from constantly hunting for their own food. Pride males probably get lazy and are less conditioned because the lionesses do most of the hunting for them. Although a river often sets a pride's boundaries, many prides cross the ones within their areas. With a healthy respect for crocodiles, Carr's lions swam whenever the occasion called for it.

In his wonderful book, *Zulu Wilderness*, Ian Player tells of a magnificent male lion in its prime that traveled for hundreds of miles from Kruger National Park to the Mfolozi Game Reserve. One of the remarkable parts of this unique story is that the lion had to cross huge rivers infested with crocodiles. It had to walk through areas where there was no game, and so had to subsist on cattle. Everyone was trying to poison, shoot, or in any way kill this cattle eater. But this lion was very smart. He traveled only at night. He never roared. He never returned to a kill, and he managed to avoid all poisoning and most shooting attempts. To the rest of South Africa, the lion became a hero, and his progress was followed in the newspapers. Finally, after six months, he arrived at Mfolozi, and he felt safe enough to roar for the first time. To the Zulus, their legendary chief, Nkosi, had come home in the form of a lion.

Checking Out the Menu, Oil on Canvas

POPULATION

Craig Packer's work led him to believe that the Serengeti, a sufficiently large, unspoiled area, could hold about three thousand lions. The population level of those lions indicated the dependence of the lions on the amount of prey available in the leanest time of the year. This is when the lions are totally dependent on the resident prey since the migratory species are gone. Wright suggests the ideal number of lions in the Ngorongoro Crater is about seventy. Lions are eminently capable of repopulating an area where their numbers have been reduced. They recovered from a plague of biting flies in the early 1960s in the crater. The seventy lions Wright describes were reduced to about fifteen in three years from this plague, according to H. Fosbrooke. In seven years they completely recovered to their former level. Cubs that would not have survived in another overpopulated hectically competitive environment, had

enough food and care to reach maturity. Packer says that when strange lions occasionally show up on the crater floor, they don't last long. No immigrant successfully settled there in the many years he studied them. He says it is a "lion factory bristling with so many teeth and claws that the traffic is all one way, up and out." Female elephants never come down to the crater floor, presumably because of all the lions and hyenas, but bull elephants are common, being too big to be bothered by anything except each other.

The Owenses found that lions could survive at least eight months with no drinking water in the Kalahari Desert. Instead of migrating in a single direction, they dispersed over very large tracts of land to find enough dry-season prey. They left the protection of the reserve not to find water, as was once suspected, but to get enough to eat. These tremendous increases in range inevitably took the prides into areas where they were in danger either from other lions, or from being shot. The Owenses observed that, unlike those of East Africa, Kalahari lionesses switched prides and pride areas frequently during the dry season. Without exception, all the lionesses they monitored associated with members of different prides. The cohesion and pride structure that were so permanent and fundamental to the social organization of Serengeti lions temporarily ceased to exist in the Kalahari population. It is an excellent example of how a species adjusts its social system to extreme environments.

The surge in human population today in most of Africa forces many lions to reside in game parks. This creates a unique problem for nomad lions. Most game parks are saturated with resident lions, forcing these nomads into surrounding cattle country, where they are shot by the cattlemen and farmers. To prevent such confrontations, some park wardens are actually culling them while they are still inside the park. Where possible, they are tranquilized and transplanted in other areas that have room for more lions. Apparently, sterilization is an option that is also being explored.

RESEARCH

There are many types of research and researchers. Some of these people are so dedicated that they pursue their work at great sacrifice to themselves and their families. They might start out looking at one aspect of an idea and pursue it relentlessly, or they may go off in another direction and come up with the most unexpected results. This whole research process is fascinating to me.

In the realm of outdoor nature study, research is just as important as it is in any other field. Schaller and Packer did much of their work at the Serengeti Research Institute, which disintegrated after it was Africanized, and the border with Kenya closed in 1977. (Back then I was delayed at that Kenya border with Tanzania by Julius Nyerere's Tanzania Green Guards, but it wasn't a problem getting through. My guide, John, demonstrated to me how, communist or capitalist, border guards are very similar, and driven by very much the same incentives. They can be made offers that they can't refuse.) Schaller's and Packer's work opened our eyes to much of the area's idiosyncrasies in general and the lion in particular. Forinstance, they discovered preferences lionesses have for a male's mane. Packer used life-sized dummies of male lions with short manes and long manes, dark manes and light manes. By calling and attracting females to the dummies, he would let them choose those in which they had the most interest. He found the females showed a preference for the darker- and longer-maned lions. Tall and dark equals handsome, at least to a lioness.

The great sculptor, taxidermist, and explorer, James L. Clark, describes how, years before Packer's discovery, he made a life-size dummy that was hollow. But he used his for decoy purposes. His friend Dugmore carried it on his back, the tall grass concealing his legs. He thus had a portable blind from which to study. Since this method of getting close was for hunting as well as photographing, and considering the obvious danger, they always carried rifles.

The very practical use of what may seem like obscure research can be readily seen in many instances. Packer, for example, relates that lions infected with the FIDV (Feline Immune Deficiency Virus) live as long as those that are not infected. Learning how the lion's immune system copes with the virus may therefore be important to human AIDS research.

George Schaller's Serengeti study was most important in that it demonstrated that lions, leopards, cheetahs, and wild dogs do not limit the population size of their prey, and it is not necessary to reduce carnivore numbers to ensure large populations of herbivores. The Serengeti could exist as an unspoiled spectacle of predators and their prey. Park wardens used to shoot wild dogs and spotted hyenas in several reserves. Jeannette Hanby and David Bygott did similar studies that con-

trasted the Serengeti lions with their well-fed counterparts in the Ngorongoro Crater of Tanzania.

Research in the 1970s, although not on lions, gave us much information about the eating efficiency of the lion's prey animals. It explained why there is so much more food available than if the prey animals were, for instance, cattle. African game ranches get much more protein per wild animal than they do from domestic cattle. Several Serengeti Research Institute scientists hypothesized that the major migratory species coexisted by specializing on grasses in different stages of growth. Dr. Richard Bell first described the grazing hierarchy of the major herbivores, and Dr. Dirk Kruelen established that herbivores on the Serengeti migrate to areas with more nutritious graze. Zebra are bulk feeders, preferring mature grasses. Wildebeest seek

any green grass. By mowing down the longer grasses, the two larger species create fresh swards of the short green grass preferred by the Thomson's gazelle. But these three species are as different as horses, cows, and sheep. How do more similar species coexist? Wildebeest, topi, and kongoni are all the same size and share a recent common ancestor, but they too divide the resources. Wildebeest prefer actively growing grasses, topi prefer intermediate grasses, and kongoni prefer senescent, older grasses. Each species gains weight most rapidly when feeding on its preferred forage.

Packer also describes the advantages of migration. The short grasses of the volcanic plains are much richer in protein, calcium, and phosphorus than the tall grasses of the northern woodlands, where mineral levels are so low that non-migratory grazers would suffer reduced fertility from phosphorous deficiency. Browsers can obtain ample minerals from tree leaves, but grazers must migrate south as soon as the rains permit.

Georgiadis's work points out the effect of migration on genetic similarity. The Rift Valley restricts the movement of several species in northern Tanzania. Wildebeest in the Serengeti and Ngorongoro crater belong to the same genetic race. But the wildebeest in the crater and Lake Manyara are as distinct from each other as separate species, even though they live only twelve miles apart. The African elephant is not bothered by mere walls or escarpments. Manyara elephants commute to the crater, for example. The genetic similarity of elephants from Kenya to South Africa implies a long history of large-scale migration.

The Citizen
Sepember 28, 1989
The National Parks Board has given instructions that all man-eating lions in the Kruger National Park must be traced and destroyed. The head of the park, Dr. Salmon Joubert, said as soon as a lion had mauled a human being it lost its fear of humans. This created a danger for employees and made it necessary to kill such lions. There is a pride of between four and six man-eating lions in the vicinity of Nwanetsi. Dr. Joubert said this unnatural state of affairs had been caused by Mozambicans, wandering through the park. A number of them had been attacked by lions. Last week, an SADF solider was mauled to death by a lion.

Sinclair found that competition between species could be measured when the abundance of one species is artificially altered. For example, if wildebeest out-compete zebra for food, an increase in the wildebeest population should cause zebra numbers to decline. Therefore, the zebra must not be seriously affected by feeding competition with wildebeest or any other ruminant. His earlier research showed that rainfall stimulates grass growth and that more calves survive when more fresh green grass is available. Any rancher could tell you the size of the wildebeest herd will depend on rain, but now they can predict what the precise number of wildebeest will be, given recent patterns of rainfall.

Other research shows that lions can count, and they most certainly can count roars. Karen McComb studied female territoriality by using playback experiments. When she played female roars to groups of different sizes, the speed with which the females arrived at the speaker depended on the odds. Play the roar of a lone female to a group of females, and a trio approaches the speaker much more quickly than a pair. Play the roars of three females to a trio, and they take as long to arrive at the speaker as a single female hearing another solitary. If the females are outnumbered, they don't approach the speaker at all.

Another use of recorded calls is for gathering information on forest lions. They obviously cannot be observed as easily as can their cousins on the plains, so a "predator" call is used. A recording of a wounded rabbit or the feeding frenzy of hyenas is played near the carcass of some bait animal. Any lions in the area are sure to appear.

There is a decades-long study of lion behavior in the Kalahari Gemsbok National Park by Professor Fritz Eloff. For more than thirty years, he has been using the remarkable tracking abilities of the San natives to reconstruct the lion's daily living habits. Although there must be parts of their daily life that cannot be learned about in this manner, the fact that there is no human disruption of the lion's normal routine gives it a very different perspective. Having seen Africans track, I can only say that I have the greatest confidence in Professor Eloff's results. His was a very unique method of research.

(Newspaper and date unknown)
ATTACKS BY BIG CATS UP, WARN RANGERS

Lions, leopards and hyenas are wild animals - with the accent on wild - and Kruger National Park rangers have recently had a number of occasions where this truism has again been proved. Research staff in the park are also more in danger. This has been brought about by the increasing number of illegal immigrants who move through Kruger from Mozambique en route to Johannesburg in search of work. They are all on foot and the animals lose their fear of man. Man is easier prey than fleet-footed antelope. Attacks have been reported from the northern parts of the park as well as at sites on the eastern boundary. "When Kruger visitors leave their vehicles to get a better look they place their lives in danger." Three illegal immigrants killed near Pafuri at the beginning of this year again highlighted this issue. Punda Maria ranger Ben Pretorius said the remains of the three would not "even have half-filled a plastic shopping bag."

THE PRIDE

A pride is a group of resident lionesses and their cubs with temporary adult males, all of which share an area and interact relatively peaceably among themselves. The foundation of the pride is the lionesses. They are all directly related, and membership is closed to lionesses from outside their group. As the females grow, they become part of this closed society. To help prevent inbreeding, males born to pride lionesses almost always leave that pride on their own or are driven out by the pride's adult males. The lionesses sometimes mate with males from neighboring prides or with nomadic males, further varying the gene pool.

Ruling males may stay with a given pride for as little as a few months or stay up to several years; they may leave of their own volition or, more commonly, be driven out by new males who then take over the pride for themselves. Pride males are frequently brothers or pride mates of similar age who were nomads before joining a pride. The number of males per pride varies with the density of the lion population. Where there are many lions, as in the Serengeti, a male needs at least one companion male to hold the pride. In areas where there are few lions, one male can keep a small pride by himself. The average size of a pride is difficult to determine, because lions often separate into smaller groups. Nevertheless, the number of lions in a pride can be as low as four and as high as the mid–thirties. Pride males may associate with nomadic lionesses, especially if these are in estrus, and pride lionesses sometimes tolerate visiting males. Males and females alike help prevent inbreeding by selectively excluding others of their own sex. Members of a pride have a general animosity toward strange lions, while nomads are much more tolerant of strangers.

There are usually twice as many females as males in a pride. This numerical imbalance is probably a result of the more adventurous lives led by the males. According to the Owenses:

> As in most species the sex ratio at birth is
> 1:1. That there are more females than

males in a population could be the result of greater mortality among young, solitary and inexperienced (specifically at hunting) males who have been forced from their natal prides, and older males who have lost their prides and who must hunt without females; intense male:male competition; and male emigration and transfer to other prides. However, the sexual imbalance within the pride is probably due to (1) male:male competition: In most habitats, a coalition numbering three immigrant male lions is optimal for conveying the most of their genes to the next generation through reproduction. Thus, resident males actively prevent additional males from joining their pride, limiting their total number to that near the optimum. (2) Males born in the pride usually emigrate, whereas most females remain in the pride for life. This will obviously lead to a bias in the sex ratio of the pride.

Packer points out that males eat more, bring in less food, and when one considers their weight, are pound for pound fairly equal with females within the pride. Prides move less during the dry season, staying near water holes or rivers because undoubtedly that is also where the prey is. In the Kalahari, where there are no water holes in the dry season, a pride's range increases as much as tenfold, because of the widely scattered prey.

One of the principal benefits of living within a pride is the protection afforded by the group. Prides are very formidable opponents to strangers. They are a community where help is provided to those individuals that may need it from time to time. Help could be in the form of fending off a stronger enemy or

Ten Lions, Oil on Canvas

acquiring food at a time when a lone individual could not hold his own. Unlike pride lions, nomadic lions form rather casual, informal groups, with animals joining and parting at irregular intervals. Solitary males have little chance of acquiring, much less keeping, a pride, so half of these males are likely to remain nomadic unless they form a companionship and take over an existing pride. Generally a companion of the same age and sex is preferred. These small nomadic groups come close to being prides, but they lack the strong matriarchal bond that defines and cements the true pride. Some lions form a permanent social unit, similar to a pride, in which they are much looser in their mutual dependence.

Schaller found that the most noticeable thing about nomads was their tolerance of each other. (But this changes when they are feeding!) This behavior seems to be directly related to their territorial imperative: They are lions, that defend no land generally, accept strangers, and are more laid back. Females, however, except when they are tending newborn cubs, generally hate to be alone for very long. In normal prides there is a great deal of touching and camaraderie. One can certainly wonder if group living is the cause or result of the lion's pride. Communal living is also practiced by wild dogs, hyenas, and other animals.

The demonstrable results of pride formation, however, do not explain why group living originally evolved. Schaller has proposed that some causes of group living have an evolutionary explanation. The evolutionary advantages of pride formation are what maximize successful reproduction in the long term. Genes of those individuals who leave the most descendants are the genes that will become widespread simply because of the larger number of descendants; this is evolutionary success.

One advantage of group living is that by hunting in groups, the lions' hunting success is greatly increased, both in numbers of animals caught and in the much larger prey that can be brought down by a group of lions. This perhaps explains why lone nomads are more accepting of strangers. .During lean times, however, as in the dry season, only small prey may be available. At that time, many lions hunt alone, and the groups that remain are much smaller. Communal groups of females are better able to protect their cubs from invaders. Another advantage of group living is the efficient use the group makes of its kills. A pride usually eats all of a kill, conserving the energy that would be needed to guard the remains. If a kill is not eaten entirely, a single lion cannot always guard the remains successfully.

On the other hand, group living can sometimes create temporary disadvantages. When food is scarce, competition within the group is fierce. Cubs frequently die of starvation during these lean periods, but adults do not. Adults who let their cubs starve rather than starve themselves apparently leave no fewer descendants in the long run, because adults compete better for food and reproduce again sooner than their offspring would have had they reached sexual maturity. Ironically, some of the harsh conditions for cubs are somewhat alleviated by the tendency of males to share carcasses with cubs, but not with females.

Incoming males evict all of the male sub-adults in their new pride. Sub-adults compete with younger cubs for food, and the new stepfathers make sure that all food goes to their own cubs. Once evicted, the young males must begin their lives as nomads.

Females usually remain in the same pride until they die. The very few evicted young females try to establish a new pride. Groups of females, on the other hand, will kill strangers in defense of their territories. This pride-type possessiveness seems to carry over into captive animals. Animal trainer Josip Marcan says that lions are much more dangerous when females are in estrus. He says the normally solitary tiger and leopard are nowhere near as affected by a female's ovulation. These other cats are no angels, of course. Evicted males stay together as a coalition after they are on their own. The larger the coalition, the better their chances to take over a new pride some day. In my opinion, the lion's immediate motivation is sex.

The Owenses, however, disagree:

> *There is no evidence or data to support the contention that the ultimate motivation for any behavior pattern is sexual pleasure. Reproductive success (in terms of the numbers of genes conveyed to the next generation) rather than sex is the ultimate payoff for the great cost to the male for gaining breeding access to females. It could be argued that sexual pleasure may be a proximate incentive, although this would be very difficult to prove. Of course, the lion does not know that reproductive success and an enhancement of his genetic fitness is the ultimate motivation for his various behaviors. Most, if not all behavior patterns have evolved (undergone natural selection) in animals (including man) because they increase the reproductive success of an individual: male springbok fight each other for territories, and the winner greatly*

Eye to Eye, Oil on Canvas

improves his opportunities to mate by control-
ling a harem of females. This greatly multi-
plies his opportunities for leaving offspring
(vehicles for his genes) in the next generation.
Since he most likely won the encounter
because of his superior resource holding
potential (he is larger, stronger, faster, has
better armament, etc.), he leaves more of his
superior genes in the next generation than
does his weaker opponent. Thus, through
time, agonistic behavior is selected for and the
genes for this behavior increase in the popula-
tion's gene pool. That does not mean, howev-
er, that the motivation for these behavior pat-
terns is the act of fighting or the act of sex. It
simply means that the individuals who
behaved in such a way "out-reproduced"
the others.

I am not a scientist, but I believe the immediate motivation for a lion taking over a pride is to have sex sooner. I just can't imagine a big male lion coming on to a lioness in heat thinking that he has to spread lion genes for the good of the species. Maybe Mother Nature is thinking of the species overall, but to me, it seems that an individual lion's instincts are just to have sex.

In taking over a pride, lions have a single focus, as was dramatically and humorously demonstrated to me in a Serengeti South tented camp in 1995. This beautiful camp is set in a kopje and the area is shared by a large pride of lions. Normally there are few problems with this arrangement. A week before I arrived, however, the pride was taken over by a new set of males. They were fighting furiously for days. One day at noon two big males came roaring and fighting right through the mess area of the camp. The waiter who described this said the cook was so terrified that he squeezed himself between the refrigerator and the freezer. There was a new couple in camp that day from California. As they were going to lunch together, the two lions came crashing through, in between the couple, almost knocking one of them over. Afterward,

the camp managers, who were concerned asked how this had affected them. Surprisingly their reply was something like, "Wow, far out, just like Disneyland!" The camp manager told me the lions had enough of their own problems without bothering with those in the camp. When I asked the waiter where he was during all this, he said "Between the refrigerator and the freezer!" That beautiful camp will always be one of my favorites. .

REPRODUCTION

Lionesses reach sexual maturity between two and a half and four years of age. Estrus, or heat, lasts from one day to three weeks. The presence of dependent young inhibits the resumption of a regular cycle. The length of intervals between estrus periods varies greatly. Some females can conceive until they die of old age. A female mates for up to six consecutive days. Intervals between matings may be as little as fifteen minutes throughout the receptive period. Brian Bertram found that females mated an average of three hundred times during each estrus, and that only one in five estrus periods resulted in cubs being born. There is surprisingly little conflict between pride males for the right to mate with a female. When two male lions court the same female, usually one gives way amicably or they share her favors.

Generally, the first male to become aware that the female is in estrus maintains undisputed possession of her. It's little wonder that there is no objection to a male's pride-mate taking over the courtship after a few days of mating fifty to seventy times a day! As fewer than one in fifteen hundred matings results in cubs being born, there is little to be gained for a male in competing violently for a female, especially if he is likely to be severely injured in the process. Bertram concluded that this inefficient mating system in lions serves a purpose other than reproduction. He presents sound arguments that this mating strategy plays an important social function, and it has probably evolved to discourage the pride males from fighting and injuring each other, which would make the pride more vulnerable to a takeover by other males. This "peace keeping" mating system helps increase the chances of survival of cubs in the pride.

The Sunday Times
October 11, 1992
TOURIST: MY BATTLE WITH HUNGRY LION
South African tourist Robert Bowler described from his hospital bed yesterday how a lion grabbed his arms in its jaws and tried to drag him from his sleeping bag. Bowler, 40, of Cape Town was treating his son, Joel, 18, of Middlesborough, England, to a canoeing safari down the Zambezi River. They were part of an eight-member group making the three-day trip from Chirundu to Mana Pools. At 4 am on Thursday — the last day of their trip — they were woken by a pride of lions which had swum across to their midstream island campsite. "I saw at least two of them," said Mr. Bowler. "I rolled over in my sleeping bag then this thing was on me. It grabbed me and tried to get me out of the bag. It took both my arms in its mouth. I shouted for our safari guide, and immediately he got a shot off. That startled the lion and it released me. Then the order was given for us to get into the boats as there were a lot of very angry lions around." Zimbabwe's Air Rescue Service flew in from Harare. Mr. Bowler, no stranger to Zimbabwe's national parks, said he has not been put off by his ordeal.

There is highly significant synchrony in the births of cubs to lionesses within a pride. Its advantages in cub survival are obvious. Cubs are able to suckle from more than one lactating female. Cubs will grow to be of similar size, with a fairly equal chance to feed at kills. Without this, larger cubs would dominate and smaller cubs would starve. With synchrony in births, more young animals will be simultaneously forced from the pride to become nomads. The larger the group of nomads to leave the pride, the greater their chances of survival. This also increases their chances of eventually obtaining their own pride area. Male lions reach physical sexual maturity at around twenty-six months. It is no surprise, then, that this is the age at which they become unwelcome within the pride. Males do not have the opportunity to mate until they have established ownership of their own pride. This "social" sexual maturity generally occurs at about five years of age.

While courting lions are mostly concerned with the obvious, they also indulge in other activities. Schaller describes how "...a male caught a gazelle and permitted the lioness to eat it. On another occasion, a lioness spotted some gazelle in the high grass nearby. She crouched and began to stalk, but the male misinterpreted the posture and mounted her. Suddenly she rushed out from under him and chased the gazelle unsuccessfully." I can well imagine.

INFANTICIDE

The behavior whereby male lions, which have just taken over a pride, will kill any cubs remaining from the previous males is referred to as infanticide. This seemingly cruel practice is nature's way of ensuring that the stronger lion's genes will be continued. Nature uses sex to accomplish this aim because females who lose their young by any means come right back into estrus. The males may now have their sex sooner.

But the Owenses disagree. "Again we disagree with your statement that sexual pleasure per se is necessarily the driving force for these behavior patterns ...Unfortunately, the term Nature does not really explain anything... It is not selected for because of sex. Sorry–the sex theory is a nice explanation around the campfire, but it is not an accurate scientific explanation as the ultimate objective."

I am certainly not challenging their premise that natural selection is at work, but that it is using the lion's sexual drive as the immediate method or incentive to further that selection goal.

Over his entire adult life, a lion may reside in a pride for no more than two or possibly three years. As Craig Packer says, "He has no time to waste being a stepfather."

Brian Bertram was the first to realize that cubs always vanished shortly after the arrival of new males in a pride. Bertram and Schaller had both seen incoming males kill cubs in the Serengeti studies, but the habitual loss of cubs implied that infanticide was a deliberate behavior rather than an aberration. The cubs in these killings were sometimes eaten. Lionesses do not take kindly to this practice, however, and although the new males usually prevail, they sometimes pay dearly. Bertram also noted the lack of litters born in the six months after a takeover, and suggests why. After such violence, stress in the females may reduce the rate of conception in matings with the new males, and females already pregnant may abort more frequently because of the presence of strange males (this also happens in mice). The successful lion's gene pool reaches future generations more quickly if the new males kill the loser's cubs. As an example, Packer describes a male that got up and charged straight at a mother and cubs. She had no choice but to run, since she was less than two-thirds his size. The male's head disappeared into the grass next to the retreating female. He pulled up one mangled cub, then the other. Two days later, the mother came into estrus and mated with the murderer. It seems to me that every lion in the wild has a father who is a murderer and a sex fiend.

MATING

Sexual activity in young lions is almost nonexistent, but they make up for it at maturity when they have their own pride.

Pause, Oil on Canvas

When they do, it is nothing but Herculean! Lions have extraordinary stamina. They go off on a honeymoon that lasts a week or so and may mate more than three hundred times.

During this time, males and females are fiercely territorial. Lions become very excited when a stranger roars in the middle of their range. Males are constantly on the lookout to keep other males away from their pride, and females are intolerant of any strange female who wanders into their territory. Should a large pride encounter a smaller one, the larger chases the smaller group out and attacks and kills any male lion they can.

A male usually stays very close to a lioness in full estrus, for she may accept several males in succession if she is not attended closely. Schaller describes one female that mated with three different males in twelve days. Either male or female may initiate copulation. He states that invitations by females outnumbered those by males by a ratio of about three to two. The average interval between matings is fifteen to thirty minutes, depending on the number of days the lioness is in heat. Believe me, I have never witnessed anything that makes that statement an exaggeration. Schaller describes a number of occasions when mating continued for more than two weeks.

Cubs

A female lion becomes secretive during her last weeks of pregnancy, and gives birth in the dense vegetation or rocks of a kopje or riverbed. She bears her cubs in places where they are fairly well hidden. Each female seems to have a preferred den site, often the spot where she herself was born. Two or three cubs will be born some 107 days after mating. At birth, lion cubs weigh only about three pounds and are almost totally helpless. Their eyes usually open between their third and fifteenth day of life. After three weeks they are able to walk.

Females often shift small cubs to different places, sometimes doing so five times in a month. They hold them with their teeth by the neck, or in the case of very small cubs, by the back and shoulders. The cubs accept this transportation passively. The cubs are extremely vulnerable to predators when the mother has to leave them to hunt. After giving birth, a mother spends most of the next few weeks alone with her cubs, but leaves them periodically to go hunting. Small cubs alone in their den make little effort to escape. Their only defense is to remain undetected. They stay hidden until they are four to six weeks old. After a certain age, however, they clearly benefit from being reared in a pride.

Cubs are separated from the rest of the pride because the lioness cannot keep up with the pride when they move while she is caring for her young. It is not that she is trying to keep the cubs from the pride. A lioness may seek out other pride members and spend the day with them, sometimes with tragic consequences. A lioness can be the most caring mother one day and the most neglectful the next. These are probably newer, inexperienced mothers.

When a lioness returns, she grunts or roars softly to gather her offspring. Schaller states that lions possess a vocal signal that means "come" but lack one that signifies "stay," except for the aggressive growl. A mother must devote all her efforts to her current batch of young. She weans her cubs when they are about six months old but does not resume breeding until her current brood becomes reasonably competent at hunting and fending for themselves. However, should her cubs die at any point before their second birthday, the mother will start mating within days. A lioness wastes no time. She has to start over and breed again. But if they survive, the cubs will have caused a very effective form of contraception: Females who don't have cubs are much less sociable. Mothers are by far the most gregarious females in the pride.

During the first two months of life, cubs subsist on milk. This is gradually supplemented with meat, which may start after the first month when the mother leads her cubs to a kill. Some incisors erupt at three weeks and canines at four. It seems unlikely that cubs feed on meat before that age. Schaller had a pet cub that ignored meat at three and a half and four weeks of age. When offered the remains of an antelope again at five weeks, however, he grabbed it, licked it, and ate some. This abrupt and noticeable change suggests that a definite maturing occurs at this age. (As a youngster, I had a young screech owl that needed to be hand-fed until in one night it caught, killed, and ate a whole mouse!)

Lion Around, Oil on Canvas

When cubs are mobile, they still tend to remain hidden until their mother returns. Full integration of cubs into the pride is a gradual and varied process. Young are not seen regularly with the pride until they are about two months old, when they are mobile enough to keep up with the moving. Two months is also the age when lionesses combine their litters, if they have not already done so. Because pride-mates communally suckle one another's young, cubs would suckle for five to eight minutes before wandering a few feet away or falling asleep at the mother's side. Most cubs end up being reared in a *crèche* formed by two to four females. Mothers nurse until their cubs are about six to eight months old, and the *crèche* persists until the mothers are ready to breed again, when the cubs are about a year and a half old.

Even when cubs are in the security of the pride, their lives depend on obtaining enough to eat. While they may have the advantages of communal suckling, in competition for nipples the smaller cubs can be shouldered aside by larger ones, creating another advantage of pride cubs being synchronized by a new male. If their mother eats before bringing them to the kill, sometimes from several kilometers away, there may be little or nothing left when they arrive. Young that are present when a kill has been made are dependent on enough meat being left for them.

At this stage of life, a cub's best chance of obtaining a meal is to follow the group. They are fully dependent on the adults for food until about a year and a half old. They may still need the help of lionesses unless they can subsist on small prey or live in areas where meat is readily scavenged. Cubs may be allowed to share meat with the males, but only if there is ample meat. Because permanent teeth enable them to compete more successfully for meat at kills, their rate of growth is now very fast. Other than occasionally allowing cubs to feed beside them, the males take no part in rearing. Paternal protection is only critical until their cubs are about nine months old. Older cubs can flee from invading males and accompany their mothers to safe haven.

Lionesses are very protective of their cubs. The only time professional hunter Fred Bartlett had lionesses come towards him or try to charge has been when they were accompanied by small cubs.

However, abandonment is the greatest cause of mortality in cubs. Schaller found that of those cubs who didn't survive, a quarter died violently, bitten to death by other lions or other predators; about a quarter died of starvation; and half simply disappeared, abandoned by their mother.

Cubs are much more playful than their elders and will rough and tumble with siblings considerably larger than themselves. They will usually play only when at least one lioness is close by. In carnivores, play is not just for fun. It is a very important melding of inherited instincts with acquired skills. Cubs are born with most of this information in their genes, but their play develops the needed abilities for bringing down moving prey. It is when cubs learn the skills of stalking, attacking, hiding, chasing, and fighting, and gain the agility that will be so important to them as adults. Playing builds bonds between siblings as well as develops their muscles. The flicking tails of normally tolerant adults are a favorite prey for cubs but at the risk of a snarl or a clout. As sub-adults, lions have limited survival skills. They now have to learn the fine points of stalking and killing by watching the adults, and by trial and error.

Concealment

Once you have encountered a lion on foot, in his own territory, on his terms, the animal is never the same to you. Meeting one without the protection of a gun or motorized vehicle is an experience that is never forgotten. It is unbelievable how an animal as large as a lion can conceal itself. On my first trip to the Ngorongoro Crater in Tanzania, I was on a slight rise looking for rhino. Back then we were not restricted to roads, and the grass was only about five to ten inches high. After lunch I was feeling safe and therefore very brave. I was about thirty feet from the vehicle, stretching, when I saw two dark almond-like objects about six inches from each other. Suddenly I realized they were the eyes of a young male lion that seemed very interested in me. I was terrified. He was about the same distance from me as I was from the car. My driver, Jon Mbuthu, firmly but calmly told me to back up slowly and not to show the lion my back. He started the engine and backed the car to me. I jumped in and did not get out again until safely up at the lodge on the rim of the crater. John never had trouble keeping me in the car after that.

The Sunday Times
June 19, 1988

SHE'S GAME TO GO AGAIN AFTER ORDEAL WITH LIONESS

Zimbabwean game rangers are combing the Zambezi Valley for a pride of lions which raided a campsite at the Mana Pools game reserve last week, severely mauling former Johannesburg secretary Debbie Smith. She was bitten through the thigh and her right calf was lacerated by a lioness's fangs. She was in an eight-member party taking a canoe trip from Chirundu to Kanyemba.

As dusk fell and the group gathered round their campfire, Zimbabwean safari guide Troy Williamson, 22, warned them that the distant growls they could hear were from prowling lions. Debbie crawled into her sleeping bag at 10:30 pm with a mosquito net suspended over her on a canoe paddle. "I woke at about 1:30 am feeling myself being wrenched, spun around and then dragged along the ground into the bush. By this time I was screaming my head off — I didn't know what it was that had grabbed me — and it must have let go. Mr. Williamson yelled at the campers not to scatter and run or they would be dragged down and the men in the party rushed up armed with paddles while the others banged gas cylinders. In the torchlight we saw there were four lions."

Victoria Falls Sacred Ibis, Oil on Canvas

Pensive, Oil on Canvas

The Sunday Times
July 13, 1986

ORDEAL OF THE LIONS' DEN

A mother of three was mauled by five caged circus lions in Pietersburg. Within seconds of grabbing her sleeve the lion had almost completely devoured her left arm. The ferocious animal was reluctant to let go as the other lions dug their claws into her back in a scramble to get at Mrs. Serfontein. But the quick action by a Mrs. Trudy Pretorius, who recently completed a first-aid course, prevented her from bleeding to death.

Associated Press
December 12, 1986

MAULED CAMPER WITH HUNTING KNIFE KILLS LION

HARARE, Zimbabwe — A burly farmer wrestled a lioness as it mauled him on the banks of the Zambezi and killed the beast with a knife thrust to the heart. Paul Bekker, indicating with bandaged hands the teeth marks under his chin and on his scalp, told how the lioness at one point had his head between her jaws. Bekker, who is 6 feet 2 inches tall and weighs 200 pounds, was on a canoe trip down the Zambezi with 15 others when the lioness attacked him in his sleep at a bivouac at Rukomechi National Park on Tuesday. He and three other members of the party were sleeping in a hut surrounded by wire mesh when the lion broke through the barrier and hurled herself onto him. "I managed to yell to the others to pass me my hunting knife, which I had hung on the wall," he said. "One of them got it to me and I stabbed the lioness in the side and back while it was biting my shoulders. Then it began chewing on my thigh and I thrust the knife into its chest three times. The third time, the blood just gushed out and I knew I had got it in the heart." The knife has a 7-inch blade. He was patched up as well as possible from the campers' medical kit, and at daybreak began the trip by canoe to the nearest staffed Parks Board camp about 10 miles downriver. "It took us several hours because we had a number of brushes with hippos," Bekker said. "They were a bit cheeky and we had to keep portaging around them."

There are as many stories about the ability of lions to conceal themselves in the bush as there are people who have been there. One day Kenya's Glen Cottar, former professional hunter, was out in the grass seeing what the game was doing. All of a sudden a lion raised its head. He saw two more and found he was surrounded by lions. He counted seven before someone brought his vehicle and scattered the cats. Cottar's equally experienced associate, Bunny Allen, tells of going with a client to sit in the shade of a large fig tree. They never made it. A pride of about eighteen lions exploded in all directions around them like a covey of quail. One almost knocked over Kikunyu, one of Bunny's trackers. A lioness passed right between Allen and his client, who were only six feet from each other! And these are experienced African professional hunters with years in the field.

On another occasion, Norman Carr's native assistant, Nelson, went out to call Carr's two pet lions in to breakfast. Carr says that Nelson was surprised to find them very close to camp. They were just sitting looking at him and he approached to admonish them when two other large lionesses stood up, having been concealed in the grass. As they advanced towards him menacingly,. three more raised themselves out of their camouflage. Fortunately, he had a shotgun which he fired over their heads...but unfortunately, it didn't work. More providentially, Nelson was from the Awemba tribe who climb trees all the time to lop treetops for their fertilizers. This ability was put to good use and after an hour or so the lions left."

Peter Davey once experienced fifteen lions concealed but resting in the grass for a whole day, literally a stone's throw from a camp full of photographers. The lions totally ignored the presence of the human beings so close to them. Davey's group had no idea the lions were there the whole day. It only became apparent when the lions decided to move in the early evening.

In his book, *Hunter's Heartbeat*, Lionel A. H. Hartley recounts having lunch with his wife, Sue, under a large shade tree. The grass was about a foot high where they were, right on the edge of the huge breeding ground of kob, a plains antelope. He went behind the tree to his car and noticed a male kob, about thirty yards away giving him the once over, almost saying, "Don't encroach on my patch." Then all hell broke loose. A lion gave a loud growl, Sue screamed, and Hartley dove into the car and slammed the door. A lioness leaped out of the grass behind the tree, going for the kob.

Hartley recounts:

How I never saw her nor why she did not take me, I don't know. We had our coffee and sandwiches and went on to find that the lioness had dragged her kill to a small gully and had four very small cubs, much to Sue's delight.

LIONS HUNTING

Before chasing prey and bringing it down to kill and eat, lions must first find and get close to it. They must hunt. Lions are very casual. A hunt can start in a deceptively relaxed fashion. While resting they will occasionally wake, sit up and look around, scanning the landscape in case something is wandering blindly into their territory unawares. The lions never appear to be in any hurry. When they start moving, looking for better hunting grounds, they set off randomly. They hunt at all times of the day and night, but in general, nocturnal hunts are more successful. Where there is little cover, most hunting takes place at night. During dry weather, lions position themselves around rivers and water holes to ambush their thirsty prey.

When lions spot game their faces become very alert and their bodies rigid. The other members of the pride are immediately alert to the opportunity. They first advance in a crouching walk, then in a crawl, belly almost touching the ground, with the head very low but above the rest of the body silhouette. They wait for the quarry to feed or look away, then sneak from one point of concealment to the next. That concealment might be grass, bushes, or rocks. If its quarry becomes suspicious, a lion can keep still for an incredible length of time. They are excellent at concealing themselves in whatever cover is available, but will always use heavy vegetation or tall grass if they have a choice. It is unbelievable how such a large animal can seem to disappear in even short grass. Crouching lions may occasionally flick their tail tips or ears.

Lions need to be close to fleet-footed prey to be successful because a rush from even a short distance may fail. They know their prey is usually faster than they are, but are also aware of their own great acceleration. Most hoofed animals have excellent peripheral vision. Prey animals have eyes in the sides of their heads while predators, including man, have eyes in the front. In heavy cover, scent alerts animals to potential danger, while sight is most important in open terrain. The lion must be close enough to its quarry to quickly accelerate to reach it before it attains its faster running speed. The prey species, of course, are very much aware of this. The greater experience of older lions makes them very good judges of the abilities of both parties. Lions may even permit part of a herd to pass before surprising less wary animals bringing up the rear. When the lion thinks it is close enough for the final rush it will wait for one more distraction before charging. Young lions tend to charge too early. Cubs benefit from watching more experienced members of the pride make a kill. To be successful they must learn the value of patience. Cheetahs and other cats will bring young or wounded animals back to their cubs to use as teaching tools. Lion cubs learn from the example of adult members of the pride.

Lions have great kinetic energy and are capable of amazing feats of strength, but their endurance in a long chase is very limited when compared with the prey they are chasing. The brief moment between the end of a stalk when the lion is like a statue and the final explosive rush is a moment of almost unbearable tension, especially since there is a life in the balance. When a lion charges its prey, it can run fifty miles an hour for about forty yards, but that is the extent of its advantage. Prey can behave in a surprisingly casual manner when lions are near. They stay as near as fifty to two hundred yards from the lion, depending on their own natural speed and acceleration. They pay little attention to resting lions, nor are they concerned with lions that have already made a kill. It is commonly thought that lions cooperate to the point that a stalk by a pride is actually planned, but this is unlikely. First, lions are notoriously careless. It is true that, as adults, they have learned that on a stalk, when they spread out, they find more game and increase their chances of coming into contact with prey. While the holding back of lions in the center of a spread of stalking lions is cooperative, it is unlikely that it is planned. (Lions have probably learned through trial and error that by letting their pride-mates extend out on the flanks the prey in front will be surrounded on three sides as opposed to just one side with a straight-forward advance.) Schaller concludes that while cooperation may be accidental, at other times deliberate cooperation does occur between hunting lions and lionesses. Communication by wildlife in the bush keeps members of the same species in contact with one another, but there is no communication of intent.

Lionesses do most of the hunting. Aside from individual hunts for themselves, males wait for females to do the work and then bully them out of the way to take over the kill.

Sometimes a lion is presented with an unexpected opportunity. It usually just grabs or pursues such prey without stalking. All big cats are opportunists and quick to take advantage of any chance encounter. However, the lion's normal method is to stalk. They often approach prey that has plenty of warning, while their companions are concealed, on the likelihood the fleeing animals will scatter straight into them.

Schaller does not think that wind direction is important to a lion, although he notes that attempts on Thomson's gazelles were three times as successful when the lions stalk upwind. I personally was surprised, but after seeing how meticulous Schaller was on his Serengeti project, perhaps there was so much game that it did not matter. I know it is very opposite the thinking of game ranger Norman Carr and most professional hunters who believe that lions will always use the wind to their advantage. In daylight, lions depend on sight more than hearing or smell, which are more important at night. Lions know full well the advantage they have when hunting in the dark. They often watch prey in the evening, but wait until dark before hunting. As described earlier, the lion's special retina has the ability to amplify light, even starlight, so that his vision is almost double that of his prey.

Rand Daily Mail
July, 1984
KENYAN AIRLIONS?
NAIROBI — Police on duty at Nairobi Airport got some unexpected reinforcements yesterday — two adult lions squatted at the main gate for three hours. Policemen at the gate retreated into their sentry box when the lions arrived at 3am and lay down on the main road to the terminal until dawn, the official Kenya News Agency (KNA) said.— Sapa-Reuters.

The Kill

The lion's attack, when observed objectively, seems like a very fast charge. That charge from the perspective of the prey seems much faster and is absolutely terrifying, if not paralyzing. My first experience of a lion coming directly towards me was at a waterhole while I was watching a wildebeest drinking. I was in a vehicle when a lioness charged right out of the grass on the opposite side of the gnu towards us both. The lioness was halfway upon us before the animal was even aware of her predicament. Even though I was in the safety of the car I had a real fright. I knew it was after the wildebeest, which it got; but my instinctive reaction was that I was the object of its charge.

I have seen this type of charge a number of times, but the most fearsome was on a hunting safari. I was accompanying a friend who was lion hunting and we were tracking one he had wounded. We knew that it was close and we were being very cautious as you can well imagine. The lion exploded out of a thicket, directly in front of us, perhaps forty yards away. The tracker leaped aside allowing my friend and the professional hunter to shoot. They did, and the animal fell three feet from them. From my vantage point, I cannot describe how much faster the lion seemed to be coming than I saw in previous attacks. I was absolutely frozen with fear. It is no wonder that some prey even freezes when facing such a frightful sight.

The kill itself depends on the size of the prey. Small animals are slapped to the ground and immediately bitten. Medium-sized prey is tackled by the forepaws pulling on the rump, knocking the animal down. Large quarry may be rammed in the side or jumped upon, with the weight of the lion's body helping to take it down. Very large animals may be hamstrung before being pulled down. The spine is bitten to paralyze its rear running machinery. If attacking from the front, a lion bites the neck. This damages a vital area in larger game, or instantly kills a smaller animal. It is also a convenient "hold" while other lions come to help, especially on big game such as Cape buffalo. In many cases, the lion will grasp the throat or neck and suffocate an animal. If the grasp is under the neck, the lion's feet may get into the act, finishing the deed much sooner. Lions may start eating their hapless quarry alive even while it is still being suffocated. Indeed most wild animals, especially in Africa, are being eaten before they are dead. It would be comforting to think such animals are in a state of shock, but having witnessed many kills, I find it hard to believe that the bleating and struggling is done by animals in shock. The Owenses guess that most feel a great deal of fear, but that a state of shock associated with the severe physical trauma may block much of the pain. Having heard the sickening bleating and cries and the plucking sounds of the claws going in and out of a zebra as the lion is trying to get a better grasp, it is hard for me to believe that they don't feel pain. When a lion takes a wildebeest or zebra out of a herd, the other animals stampede to escape the attack, but very soon pull up and look around. On seeing that the lions have all they want, they begin grazing again as though nothing had happened. They know that they are safe from further attack. Unlike some predators, lions kill only to eat or in self-defense.

In his findings in 1972, Schaller provided scientists the data to estimate the amount of prey killed by lions hunting in different sized groups. Apparently, pairs of lions garnered the most food each day. Although a successful pair would always have to divide its spoils in two, pairs succeeded twice as often as singles, and sometimes caught multiple prey. A third member did not help the group's hunting success enough to justify its presence.

Diet

In some areas, lion prides have become specialists in killing one particular species. For example, in Gorongoza, Mozambique, Schaller describes animals which frequently killed adult hippo while they were grazing at night. This is unheard of in most areas where these animals commonly occur together. Lions, however, will eat just about anything when hungry. Crocodiles, plains game from dik-dik to buffalo, birds, insects, snakes, fish, and even fruit are all on a lion's menu. They will eat whatever they have to. The lion's diet changes drastically in desert areas during dry seasons. The Owenses describe Kalahari lionesses that had to travel from five to ten miles almost every night to find food. The males had to

2 Lions in Grass, Oil on Canvas

spend more time apart from their females and did much more of their own hunting.

Lions' preferred prey is large antelope, zebra, buffalo, and warthog. Selection of food depends mainly on what is at hand, be it controlled by time of season or the abundance of the area. The larger the animal they can take down, the more there is for the pride. Although quite dangerous, buffalo provide so much meat that they seem to be worth the risk of counterattack. In regions where alternatives are plentiful, however, they rarely hunt buffalo. It is not worth the risk to challenge such formidable quarry. The extreme price of making an error also limits the attempts made on hippo, rhino, and baby elephant. Small prey, on the other hand, requires too much work for the small amount of food that results. The more abundant a prey species is, the greater its chances of being taken. An adult male lion requires approximately eighteen pounds of meat per day, and a female lion about twelve pounds.

Buffalo weigh a thousand pounds or more, and they are very aggressive, dangerous animals. They killed many of the lions Packer was working with in the Serengeti. During his stay, they also gored several rangers and children. His own two adult children are more frightened of buffalo than of lions. Most professional hunters consider buffalo the most dangerous of the dangerous game. Smaller groups of female lions also seem scared of buffalo, but the Owenses told me that lion prides of five or six members in the Luangwa Valley often kill adult buffalo. Packer says very large prides seek them out but attack with great care, encircling the beast, jumping on its back, and steering clear of its thrashing horns. A successful buffalo hunt requires great care even by lions. Carr says that lions in northern Zambia and the Luangwa feed almost exclusively on buffalo, about seventy-five percent. Solitary females may get enough to eat, but their world is filled with challenges. They will first feed on liver, spleen, and all the soft parts that can be eaten fast, in case other predators arrive. Old lions are capable of taking up the oddest diets; they catch mice, frogs, lizards, and guinea fowl, and even follow hyenas around in hope of snatching carrion.

Carr described a lioness holding down a struggling wildebeest while her adolescent cubs ate chunks of living meat from it while the animal was still struggling. He also believed lions are cannibalistic. Once, when baiting a cattle-eating trio, he shot one at night. He waited before turning the light on the remaining two lions so as not to disturb them. When he did turn it on, he found the lions eating their just-shot comrade instead of the dead cow.

Man is certainly not excluded from the lion's diet. Killing humans is much easier than chasing and killing their normal prey, and once this discovery is made, so are additions to the local obituary columns. More on this later.

FEEDING AT KILLS

It has always surprised me how such a social cat like the lion can be so nasty while eating. Lions that are very tolerant, even affectionate, of each other most of the time become aggressive and possessive at feeding time. Weaker animals must wait while stronger members bolt their meat, snarling at and clouting anyone threatening their portion. To do otherwise raises the prospect of very stern consequences. But then these cantankerous lions make up by engaging in an elaborate face-licking and head-rubbing ritual after they finish eating. By the time they have washed all the gore from one another's faces, peace has been restored to the group. It is an excellent example of nature's strongest always being taken care of first, ensuring continuation of those genes. Males will pinch a small carcass from a female unless, perhaps, she is in estrus. Lions that are completely gorged will still chase vultures and hyenas. In Botswana a guide and his clients reported of photographing a gorged lioness feeding just inches from a hyena.

Despite being completely sated, lions can still be the embodiment of greed. Males, especially, have been seen, bulging at the belly, jealously guarding a kill it would be impossible for them to eat any more of, and in some instances dragging a huge, heavy pile of remains into thick cover to hoard. A fight between lions is a very violent affair. Read George Schaller's very poignant description of the result of a fight involving two big males:

Encrusted with blood, his body (was) covered
with punctures and cuts. A deep gash
angled across his brow, closing one eye, and
a fist-sized hole penetrated his chest. Tatters
of his golden mane littered the area, mute
evidence of a titanic struggle. He breathed
with difficulty. Then suddenly the victor
emerged from a nearby thicket and slowly
walked up to the defeated one. He gazed
down at him and received a faint growl...and
returned to the remains of a zebra, which
may have been one cause of the dispute.
Almost imperceptibly, life ebbed from the
wounded male. His breathing became feeble,
his bladder emptied, and finally his pupils
grew very large. I felt almost ashamed for
intruding on the freedom of his last moments
as the amber fires
faded from his eyes.

Like the rest of us, lions usually take the path of least resistance in everything. So it is when eating. They will start at the soft rear end and underbelly, usually before the poor creature is dead. They eat the brisket out and continue up the ribs and into the chest cavity. They will take all the easy-to-eat organs, and then the muscles. From there they finish off the meat that is attached to the bones. When the male's hunger is satisfied, the rest of the pride can start their feast. At this point there is a terrifying noise of snarls and crunching flesh and bones as the lions hungrily finish off the kill. Jackals will dash in and snatch mouthfuls, as quick as lightning. It astonishes me how fast a pride can make a carcass disappear, even with the males keeping the females off until they are well satiated. Lions will drink deeply after eating.

After they have had their fill, lions like to get on to their midday naps. They can be very tolerant of the blistering midday sun and the ever-present ticks and flies. They also look so peaceful and affectionate. Younger animals may play with their favorite toy, an adult's tufted tail. It's hard to believe that they seemed ready to violently kill each other just a short time before at the kill. Because food may be scarce at times, predators are capable of gorging themselves to grotesque proportions. According to Schaller, a lion can consume as much as a quarter of its weight and a hyena as much as a third, in a single eating frenzy!

Lions can take a good bit of time digesting their food. Carr shot a man-eating lion with human remains on which it had fed five days previously still in its stomach. He knew it hadn't eaten anything since because he had been spooring (tracking) it continuously during that period of time. He considers five days without eating a long time, but this particular animal wasn't unduly thin.

SCAVENGING

Lions, like all the big cats, are opportunists. They will readily use intimidation to scavenge any kill they come upon on. This is often an important source of food for them, especially single lions. Conversely, they can just as easily lose a kill if they leave it unguarded or are outnumbered by hyenas. Hyenas are excellent hunters, and male lions sometimes rely on them to find a kill. Schaller's study showed that plains lions scavenge almost three times as much as the woodland cats. On the plains, they can see vultures above a carcass from several miles away. Hyenas, which provided many of the carcasses, are more common there. Wild dogs and cheetahs, and to a lesser degree leopards, provide additional free meals. Bunny Allen describes watching a lion pride drag a zebra into heavy brush, then scraping away any signs of blood and other evidence to keep vultures from finding it while they digested the first zebra that was already in their bellies.

The pecking order at a kill descends from lions to spotted hyenas, to wild dogs, then to brown hyenas, cheetahs, and jackals. Leopards usually avoid all this by taking their kill up into a tree. While lions normally kill only as much as they need to eat, they will occasionally kill far more than they need. This probably occurs by accident in instances where unnatural circumstances put prey

Etosha Chase, Oil on Canvas

in front of lions on a "silver platter." This indicates the killing instinct is not dependent on hunger alone.

A pride of up to twenty lions needs several zebra or wildebeest a night. Tony Dyer thinks that memories of hungry times can make wanton killers of both lions and leopards. He maintains that lions have been seen to kill up to fifteen Thomson's gazelle or impala in one successful ambush, and eat only very few of them.

COMPETING PREDATORS

Predators of all kinds weed out the sick, wounded, and old, keeping grazing herds healthy and alert. They chase the game, thereby spreading out the gene pool, which helps to reduce inbreeding. They are very effective at enhancing the survival rate of stronger, more fit individuals, who will leave more offspring in the ensuing generations. When two species of predators are competing for the same prey, they will not tolerate each other; they try to kill each other, without provocation, given any opportunity.

HYENAS

In my opinion, hyenas and lions absolutely hate each other. This is not the opinion of scientists like the Owenses.

> As scientists we prefer to avoid such terms as "hate" which are anthropomorphic and loaded with human connotations. We realize that you are not writing a scientific treatise, but we would recommend that you also avoid these terms. Certainly lions and spotted hyenas are keen competitors, but this does not prove that they "hate" each other any more than a lone wildebeest hanging out with gemsbok implies that they "like" the gemsbok. Solitary wildebeest males often join herds of other species because they are safer in a herd (selfish herd theory). We can measure how successful they are in and out of herds, and can thus quantify the value of living in a herd. We cannot measure how much a wildebeest "likes" a gemsbok. In the same vein, we can measure how often hyenas and lions, or other carnivores, compete for food. They may fight, chase, attack, eat, or otherwise behave as though they "hate" each other, but we have no way of knowing whether or not they "hate" each other in the human sense. Almost certainly they do not. We cannot measure or prove how they are feeling, but we do know that they exhibit agonistic behavior in competition for resources. Feelings akin to our own may drive this behavior—but as yet we cannot know or measure this.

Nevertheless, their fights have been seen by most of us who have been fortunate enough to spend time in Africa. They certainly have been documented on many television programs on animals. Lions at their kill may allow jackals access to their meat, perhaps because they are so nimble and only seem to grab small scraps anyway; but it would normally be sudden death for any hyena that might approach too close.

Hans Krunk and Lawrence Frank describe spotted hyenas commuting regularly with the migratory herds. A female hyena may travel fifty miles before reaching her prey, then spend several days feasting before returning to deliver milk to her cubs. After nibbling at morsels of stringy meat, tendons, and sinew, the Owenses describe a brown hyena opening her jaws wide, crushing leg bones as thick as baseball bats and swallowing splinters at least three inches long. These were measured later by fecal analysis. These hyena droppings are a very important source of calcium for many animals, especially antelope and giraffe.

Because they must forage alone, yet rear their young communally, brown hyenas are a curious blend of the social and the solitary. The Owenses describe communal suckling in brown hyenas.

This had been seen in a few other wild carnivores, including lions and wild dogs, but had never before been recorded in hyenas. Adoption occurs often in brown hyenas. In the period during which the Owenses watched one den, 70 percent of the cubs that survived were adopted orphans. Spotted hyenas will displace brown hyenas at carcasses.

Hyenas often steal from quite formidable competitors including leopards. Apparently it is too risky for a leopard to fight a hyena. The hyena's massive shoulders and neck absorb many bites and slashes, whereas a single crushing bite from the hyena could break the cat's leg, or even kill it. Losing a carcass is far less costly than the certain death that would follow from losing the use of a leg.

LEOPARDS

Leopards are not like lions socially; they are loners. With the exceptions of mothers with cubs and mating pairs, they are always alone. I did once see two big leopards share a warthog in a tree, but they fed alternately and were probably two large young siblings hanging out together right after leaving the mother. A leopard in lion country is always alert to the presence of his larger cousin. They both prey on and compete for smaller antelope and warthog as well as other animals. Like most birds and beasts of prey they are very intolerant of other predators.

CHEETAHS

Hyenas not only dominate leopards they also chase cheetahs from their kills. Cheetahs are less powerfully built than leopards, and much more timid. Cheetahs can even leave a carcass because of vultures. This is probably because they are more concerned with the other predators that vultures could attract than with the vultures themselves. Somewhat similar to lions, cheetahs are social, although female cheetahs don't form permanent groups. They are often seen in pairs or family groups. Outside Kruger National Park I saw six animals that appeared to be a mother with five sub-adults. I was surprised at such a large number but U. Pienaar, who wrote so much on the animal life of Kruger National Park in South Africa, records family groups as high as eight.

Cheetahs are much gentler than lions. Whether cubs or adults, they just never seem to quarrel, unlike lions with their constant bickering, especially at a kill. I suppose that when you live in a world where most other predators push you around, you can get mellowed out. Cheetahs specialize in chasing gazelle on the open plains. They would have an extremely hard time in heavily treed areas. They are fast, very fast. Cheetahs can easily catch a terrified Thomson's gazelle. And the running gazelles you see in a game park or on television are nothing compared to one that is running for its life right in front of you. The screen just cannot give the viewer the scale that is so necessary to appreciate such velocity. I had a few occasions when some of these chases came within yards of me. I just do not have the ability to describe to you how fast they are; both predator and prey. Cheetahs can easily reach sixty miles an hour, and according to Demmer, have reached over seventy on a racetrack. The cheetah's sprint is so fast that its success rate is equaled only by wild dog packs whose forte is cooperative endurance. Cheetahs have far less problem catching a gazelle than keeping it. Being lower on the pecking order, other predators often seize their prey. Lions, hyenas, leopards, and wild dogs kill most cheetah cubs.

TIGERS

Although tigers only compete with the very small Indian lion population and are not on the African continent, the inevitable argument arises as to the comparative ferocity and killing powers of the lion and tiger. Author John Taylor, one of the most experienced of all the African hunters, argues that tigers are known to kill larger prey by themselves, while lions only rarely pull down exceptionally large prey on their own. He feels this proves the tiger must be both stronger and a better killer than the lion. There is, however, considerably more game per lion in Africa than there is per tiger in India. Unlike the solitary tiger, the African lion has never had to devise methods of killing larger beasts such as elephant and rhino by itself. The tiger's favorite method of hunting is to ambush larger prey and spring on their shoulders, close thier teeth on the back of the neck and bite, at the same time as one mighty-muscled forearm grabs the animal by the nose and wrench-

Sun Spots, Oil on Canvas

es the head around. This can sometimes break the neck, where-upon death is instantaneous. Lions and tigers have been put into pits together in the past. The outcomes were apparently mixed since the much heavier Siberian tiger wasn't used. Its one-hundred- pound-or-more advantage would give it quite a plus in Las Vegas.

PHOTOGRAPHING LIONS

Photographing lions or any other dangerous game from blinds can be not only conducive to great shots, but ver, exciting. Today, of course, almost everyone gets their photos from a vehicle. This may be a bit wobbly if it is windy, but it is certainly smart. In the early part of the last century, some photographers would bury themselves in a thorn *boma*. A few of these brave souls even did it at night. I guess in those days the primitive equipment and conditions made the early African explorers and settlers a lot like our American fron-tier people. Although I've done some very stupid things to get a good sketch or photograph, I definitely prefer the relative safety of a *machan* (an elevated platform or blind fixed in trees), or the steel security of a motor vehicle.

In Africa, I have spent a number of nights in *machans*. These nights are pure magic with the booming of frogs, choruses of insects, and hoot of an occasional owl. If you're near hippo water, their pon-derous grunting can even make the machans vibrate. But to hear the roar of an African lion at night is a primordial spell, especially when you're not on the ground, but within feet of a lion.

Old-time stalwart photographers would not be so secure. They would set themselves by a kill specifically to get photos of lions din-ing just a few feet away or stalking about the *boma*, which is really ridiculously fragile. Their heartbeats must have felt like muffled tom-toms. Can you imagine refilling the flash powder in the midst of a feeding frenzy?

LOVING LIONS AND HUNTING THEM

Different people exhibit love for animals in different ways. Thomas Dinesen concluded in his book, *My Sister Isak Dinesen*, that "the lion for Tanne (Karen Blixen, who wrote as Isak Dinesen) was the symbol of Africa." She herself was one of the great writers of her time. In *Out of Africa*, she described her unforgettable memo-ries of days and nights of lion hunting when, in lonely, wild, bush country, she would spend the hours of tropical darkness:

> *in suffocating suspense, crouching behind a fragile thorn boma scarcely daring to breathe, waiting for the lion or lions to come and take the stinking bait set out for them and when the time between sunset and sunrise seemed like fifty years. One feels that lions are all that one lives for... In their build, posture, movements and size, lions have a majesty which inspires fear in one and makes one think later that every-thing is so small.*

She made "an honest apology to hunters whose ecstasy over hunting I had never before understood. There is nothing in the world quite like it." Karen Blixen and Denys Finch Hatton hunted many lions together and chose a future burial place for Hatton up in the Ngong Hills overlooking her farm. They had an almost mystical perception of the lion. After she left Africa, Gustav Mohr wrote her of a strange thing that had happened by Hatton's grave after he was buried. "The Masai," he wrote, "have reported to the District Commissioner at Ngong, that many times, at sunrise and sunset, they have seen lions on Finch Hatton's grave in the hills. A lion and a lioness have come there and stood, or lain, on the grave for a long time."

Most friends of mine who consider themselves hunters don't hunt just to kill, but kill to have had the completed hunting experi-ence. In her book *Encounters with Lions*, Jan Hemsing says it was a curious fashion among some of the early hunters, including the male and female non-professionals (such as Karen Blixen and oth-ers) that they become very sentimental over their kills. Watching their victims slowly die, or even embracing them in death, seemed to be the ultimate experience of their hunt.

A story has it that when an argument took place in the bar of the Norfolk Hotel between elephant hunter Steve Schindelar and another hunter, Schindelar was told tightly: 'One more word out of you, Fritz, and you'll be dying in my arms." Such sentiment is diffi-cult for most of us to understand.

Angel's Chase, Oil on Canvas

LION-MAN CONFRONTATIONS

Winston Churchill said there is nothing more exhilarating than to be shot at without effect. I can certainly add that you are never so alive as when something is trying to kill you. I have watched many lions from vehicles, and too many on foot. It's very easy to take them for granted and let their apparent disinterest in jeeps deaden your fear of them. It's a mistake. Any lion, no matter how docile looking, has those terrible instinctive reflexes waiting to explode at what is sometimes the most innocuous stimulus.

Lion confrontations vary from the humorous to the very deadly. There was an African woman named Mrs. Marula who would chase lions off a kill with nothing but a stick (and apparently no fear at all) simply because she wanted the meat for herself. Again this was in an area where the local people did not tolerate lions and they constantly put pressure on the cats. Even today, in some parts of Africa, tribesmen will chase lions from their kill (once they feel the lions have almost satisfied their hunger) and take away the rest of the meat. These tribes get away with it so often that they just consider it another way to get food. Clive Cowley, writing on the River Bushmen of the Okavango Swamps, says the little, pygmy-sized people will also rush at gorged lions and rob them of their prey.

People who live with or study lions all their lives—zoo curators, for example—emphasize their utter unpredictability, even in captivity. Many feel that "it is the lion you trust most that is likely to lash out one day with very unfortunate consequences." I suppose lions are very much like us in that respect, some being much more aggressive than others. A friend, told me of walking into a pride of lions. that were in grass at the edge of a dry riverbed. Each time he and his guide, Rob Styles, tried to retreat, the lions would crawl toward them. The tension must have been unbearable, since this went on for more than a half-hour. Just before dusk, the men finally reached the other side of the riverbed, disappeared behind some rocks, and made their way back to camp. Self-defense in such situations is usually all but impossible, even if you see the attack coming, and lions stay alive by making sure that you don't see them coming.

When it comes to lions, the behavior of camp staff varies from country to country. In Kenya and Tanzania, most camp staff come from villages where hunting lions to protect livestock was a necessity, and as a consequence have little fear of them. If they had a lion in camp, they were liable to turn out to enjoy the fun, throw a few sticks and things, and generally have a good time. In camps where the staff's villages were not in the habit of challenging lions, they were terrified when lions were close.

When Bill York was twenty-two years old, he had been in Kenya fighting Mau Mau terrorists for about two years. He had been wounded by a terrorist and had lost the use of his right hand. He went to the Northern Frontier District of Kenya with his friend, John Chapman, for a break. Their intention was not to hunt, except for the pot, but merely to wander around, photographing game, doing a bit of fishing in the river, and generally loafing about. The area was trackless except for the game trails. Human population was scarce and almost non-existent away from the river. Wildlife was numerous, from elephant down to the tiny dik-dik. There were many predators so protecting their ponies was a significant chore. There were only the two men so it was undesirable to build a thorn *boma* every night. "In any case I have never known a thorn boma of whatever height or thickness to be a proof against determined lion." York wrote: "Our intention was to string rope around camp about two feet above ground and attach camel bells at intervals and if the bells went off we would awaken and fire a couple of shots into the air. This would be sufficient to drive them off, or so we hoped."

While picking up some drinks in a village, they were told that a pride of lions had moved into the area a short time before and had killed a camel and a few goats. Apparently this pride was not intimidated by man and had driven off the herders who attempted to protect their stock.

I asked if they had contacted the Game Warden in Isiolo, George Adamson. Since Isiolo was about fifty miles away, across bush and desert country, their reply was

Expensive Meal, Oil on Canvas

understandably, in a negative. They asked if we would hunt and kill the offending lion. Apart from the fact that we were enjoying ourselves doing nothing we were not adequately armed for a lion hunt. Both John and I carried 12 gauge shotguns and I had a 6.5mm Mauser rifle. These were weapons intended to merely secure food for the pot, not to deal with marauding lion. It was somewhat embarrassing to refuse but we dealt with the embarrassment manfully. Next morning we departed shortly after first light.

The two men took a game trail that led to a waterhole some sixty miles away. Standing near the waterhole were some giraffe and Grant's gazelle, looking very alertly at something in the bush to the left of the trail.

We sharpened our senses, it is no fun being the potential prey of something one cannot see. As we approached the waterhole the giraffe and gazelle ran off. Suddenly, out of the bush, exploded a pride of lions. Within seconds they were circling around us, I was astonished at their temerity, particularly at mid day in bright sunshine. Our ponies panicked and started off at a gallop, with John and I clinging on as best we could. The pride was in pursuit, but obviously more in play than earnest, they could have easily have overtaken us and grabbed the ponies. After careening along for a hundred yards or so I managed to get a grip on my pony and pull out my shotgun. A couple of shots fired in the general direction of the lion pride dissuaded them from following further and we managed to stop and quieted our scared ponies. Believing that by nightfall we would

be out of the pride's range we began to enjoy the rest of the day. Not wanting to risk our ponies after the scare of the morning we erected our rope enclosure and cut a bunch of dry grass for them to feed on. While John settled camp and started a fire I climbed a low rocky hill to scan our surroundings. Looking down on our campsite imagine my horror when I saw a pride of lions padding along our trail, they looked very much like the animals that had caused our fright of the morning. What a dilemma! The pride was obviously bent on mischief, if they were merely hungry they could have easily secured food from the abundant antelope we had seen during the day. Why were they following us?

They took some precautions and built two fires between the perimeter rope and the tethered ponies and a third for themselves. They heard lions roaring in the distance and hoped that the pride had finally left them. Towards dawn, Bill was awakened by a grunting lion around the camp. He switched on a flashlight and saw a lioness inside the rope; the camel bells had not clapped out so she had obviously spotted the rope and simply jumped over. At that point she had not grabbed a pony so he fired a shot over the lioness' head. The loud bang scared her off, followed by the rest of the pride. Unfortunately, the bang of the shotgun scared the ponies even further. One of them broke his tethering rope and disappeared. Dawn came and to their amazement, the lost pony was grazing about a hundred yards away. They recovered their pony and decided to put some distance between themselves and the lions. They moved onto the crest of a rocky ridge which rose about a hundred feet above the surrounding country.

Within minutes of lighting a fire we heard lion roars not too far away. We sincerely hoped that these were local lion and not those which had been following us. This night I loaded my 6.5 with hard nose bullets, no

More Lawyers, Oil on Canvas

*more shots in the air, I intended to shoot any
lion that came around the camp. Shortly
after our evening meal we heard distinct
sounds of scratching and grunting, evidence
that lion were climbing the rock. Waiting
until the sounds were really close I switched
on my flashlight, and lo and behold! There
were several lion padding around. The closest animal was a large female, I planted a
shot into the heart region and she sprang
into the air and then slithered down the
slope. The other members of the pride bolted
and we were left nervously flashing the light
in all directions in case they returned.
During the remainder of the night we sat listening to roars and grunts from the pride
emanating just beneath us.*

The next morning the only lion sign was the partially eaten
carcass of the lioness Bill had shot. After carefully scanning the
surrounding bush they packed their gear and headed off again.
They did not see any more of the lions that had persistently followed them for a period of two days and nights.

*I had never been able to explain satisfactorily
the behavior of that pride. Ponies, I know,
are delectable prey but that cannot explain
such persistent pursuit. That it was the
same pride that followed us is unquestion-
able, the lioness I shot had some shotgun pel-
lets in her hide. Since the only time I actually fired a shotgun directly at them was at our
first meeting I could only conclude that it
was the same.*"

Bill concluded that following four ponies (two for supplies) and
two men was as good as any way for the lions to spend their time.

Former Uganda PH, Brian Herne believes that lions in the
Kalahari are much more aggressive than those in East Africa. We
have had many conversations on this. In my experience, Kalahari
lions certainly seem to be bolder, perhaps because it is tougher surviving in the Kalahari than on the game-filled plains of East Africa.

I would think that anything as easy to catch as a human
would easily fit on a Kalahari lion's menu when times are tough in
the dry season. George Schaller agrees with Elizabeth Thomas,
who says that "*... lions who have no fear of people, who by tradition
do not expect people to be dangerous, are the dangerous ones.*"

Most African hands consider tents to be very good protection
from predators at night — including, of course, lions. I have
always thought so myself. On a recent safari in the southern part
of the Serengeti, I was awakened by a very muffled *thump, thump,
thump.* Unless it is unbearably cold, I always have the tent flaps
up so I can enjoy the African night much more. This night was no
different, and there was only mosquito netting between me and
that African night. I turned my head in my cot and saw a lioness
three feet from me, lying down gently thumping her tail on the
mosquito netting. At the time it was very exciting. Curiously, what
I remember most was the absolutely putrid smell of her breath.
After doing the research for this book, I now realize the graveyards
have more than their share of like-minded people who were
dragged from their tents and killed. A professional hunter, Peter
Hankin, was killed by an old, crippled lioness in the Luangwa
game reserve in 1974. She jumped through the fly of his tent,
landed on him, and most probably broke his neck, killing him. She
then dragged his body into the bush and was feeding on it when
shot and killed by Jou Joubert, a professional hunting in the area
with client Samuel Lehner, who was the father of a friend of mine,
George Lehner.

Lionel Hartley had a harrowing experience while trying to put
an end to a lion that had eaten eight people near Baragoi. Unlike
many man-eaters, this one had also eaten livestock during its
eight-person killing spree. Hartley awoke one morning to find that
the lion had circled his fly-tent. These are very flimsy, portable
tents in which both the hunter and client sleep while away from
the main camp. The huge lion's tracks were only six feet away.

East African Denis Lyell says the lion is especially dangerous
"because he is difficult to see on account of his cover, and he can
hide behind a tuft of grass; is quick in his movements when he
wants to come into action, will likely charge if too closely
approached, and wounds from him are always septic."

My Masai tracker, Bwowae, told me that a lion's most dangerous weapon is neither his teeth, nor his claws perse, but what are called his dewclaws. These claws roughly correspond to a human thumb, and are about two inches long. They are curved and very sharp. The dewclaws are usually kept folded against the lion's front legs (wrists) and are difficult to see, but the lion can extend them at will so they stand out almost at right angles. They are used for slashing, and these terrible hooks can disembowel a man with one blow.

In another incident, Tony Henley, an honorary game warden in Kenya, Tanzania and Uganda, told me of a lion that had caught a Bushman by his leg. Fortunately for the Bushman, his wife had beaten the lion over the head with a burning log and driven it off. He was not badly injured and they dressed his wounds and gave him an antibiotic. The lioness next turned up in a camp called "James's Camp" some thirty miles away and killed a Bushman woman during early evening. The hunter in charge of the camp, Burt Milne, was able to shoot the lioness. It turned out to be a very old animal with no teeth and in very poor condition. As I understand it, the woman died from the infections. Many deaths by lions are the result of these open sores. There is great danger of infection to any survivor of an attack, because the lion's claws and teeth carry a great deal of filthy, compacted, decaying flesh and dirt, which is left in the deep, trench-like wounds.

Henley also described to me an incident when a wounded lion knocked him down. With the lion crunching his shoulder and tearing at his elbow and biceps, Tony decided the only thing left for him to do was to play dead. The lion stopped biting him and just lay on top of him breathing heavily. Tony said that he was hoping the lion would die before he did. He had been in this position maybe ten minutes or so, when he saw his Land Rover approaching, driving very slowly in his direction, with several people brandishing rifles in the back. He had previously lost two of his friends, Henry Pullman and Roy Windham; they had both been shot and killed while being mauled by a lion, so when the car stopped he screamed at them to shoot the lion in the head. Fortunately for Tony, they did. But that was just the beginning of his suffering.

The next week was hell, as the wounds all poured pus through drains, and they filled me up with antibiotics. My right arm swelled up to a gigantic size, turned a horrible blackish color, and gave me a terrific amount of pain until one of the night nurses started to apply hot poultices every few hours. That brought the swelling down very quickly and I felt much better.

Robin Hurt has had many experiences with lions. He wrote to me about the following incidents and thoughts on lions:

Over the years, I have had lion in camp more often than I care to remember. Mostly they pass through and the incident has been of little consequence, apart from a pleasurable experience. Occasionally, though, the nocturnal visit of lions in camp has led to much excitement. On one occasion a pride of lion established themselves in the centre of my Kigosi camp for several days and practically brought the camp to a standstill, with the camp staff seeking refuge most of the time in the back of a seven ton truck. No showers, late meals, and general pandemonium—a most unsatisfactory state of affairs! All efforts to get the lions to leave camp failed, and mostly just made matters worse by provoking tempers and lots of demonstrative growling, grunting and lashing of tails. Short of shooting, which we didn't want to do, there was little that could be done until eventually, we induced the animals to leave camp by dragging a buffalo carcass through the camp, and successfully attracted them away with this free meal! Another time, a lion tried to kill a bull buffalo in the middle of camp. A buffalo careening around with a lion on his back can do unbelievable damage in the dark. The guy ropes to my tent were snapped and before I could collect my wits and my rifle, the tent collapsed completely on top of me. The buffalo somehow managed to

Spooked, Oil on Canvas

get away alive but no doubt had many scars to show from the fracas. I came out of the tent badly shook up and feeling a bit of a twit!

Another time I was fly camping in the Serengeti, under the stars without tents, when two big male lion chose to parade and roar right through the camp. My lady client and her new husband were rudely awakened by the duet of lion roars at four or five yards distance. The wife screamed for the husband's help, but all he did was cover his head with the blankets and silently sink deeper into his bed. The result of this incident was the beginning of the end of that marriage! For, as the lady told me the next morning, what good is a wimp as a husband? My bed was situated a hundred yards or more from them, for obvious reasons, and I didn't completely believe the story as I thought the lions had passed by further afield. I was convinced, however, when I saw the tracks near their beds. Happily, the woman's screaming and shouting unnerved the lions and they decamped in haste!

Here is a supposedly true story that I have heard a number of times. A very tough old Afrikaner (of Dutch descent) farmer, who had a lion as a pet, used a whip to control it. One day he found it near the chicken coop and beat the hell out of it, since chickens were off limits. After disciplining the lion he went inside and there, reclining by the fireplace, was his pet lion. He had just whipped a *wild* lion! I have not been able to document this one so it goes in this book as a tall story. However, for those of you who have had any experience with those tough old Afrikaner farmers, you may agree that such behavior is right in line with what one might expect.

In his book *Man-Killers I Have Known*, A.J. Siggins describes a Dutchman who came upon six aggressive big lions and killed five of them. The sixth charged and caught him trying to reload. He

died in Enkeldoorn hospital. Siggins also tells of telegrams that were received regularly from stationmasters at the turn of the twentieth century, such as this one from Simba Station, August 17, 1905: "Surrounded by two lions while returning from distant signal and hence pointsman went on top of telegraph post near water tanks. Train to stop there and take him on train and then procee., Traffic manager please arrange." And from Tsavo Station, April 20, 1908: "Driver to enter my yard very cautiously, points locked up, no one can get out. Myself, shedman, porters all in office. Lions sitting before office door."

Safari guide, author and photographer, Alan Binks, describes in Jan Hemsing's *Encounters with Lions* an evening when they were surrounded by lions deep in the Selous Game Reserve. They started throwing stones at the lions to move them along. All they got in reply were some spine-chilling growls as the lionesses changed their positions, all the while looking at them intently.

At about this time a word began to impinge on my subconscious and refuse to be submerged again— man-eaters! We were about as far into the reserve as we could be, a long way from the nearest motor track and there hadn't exactly been a lot of prey species for the lions in the area as far as we had seen. There were, we knew from the evidence we had seen, poachers in the vicinity and it was quite possible that the odd one could have fallen prey to these lions, living rough as they did in their small camps full of drying meat and skins. As far as we knew, these lions could have learned the habit of getting their food from these camps and were now looking at us with exactly this thought in mind. Imagination was not lacking in our camp this night. We threw more stones. We got more ferocious growls and one of us was sure that one of the lions was sneaking round the side for a flank attack. This called for drastic measures, so we now started throwing burning pieces of wood from the fire at the lions.

Zebra at Etosha Pan, Oil on Canvas

Beware Below, Oil on Canvas

The Citizen
January 3, 1997

TWO ARE EATEN BY LIONS IN KRUGER

PUNDA MARIA, Northern Province — Two illegal immigrants were eaten by lions as they tried to cross through the Kruger National Park from Mozambique into Northern Province, park officials said yesterday. The woman and a child, part of a group of nine illegal immigrants who were waiting for the moon to come up before continuing their journey, scattered when an elephant bull surprised them. They had been sitting next to the tar road between Shingwedzi and Punda Maria near the Mandadzidzi Windmill on the night of December 30. The rest of the group heard the woman and child screaming. The group got together the next day and told tourists of their ordeal. The tourists reported it to game ranger Ben Pretorius at Punda Maria near Louis Trichardt. Mr. Pretorius said he found the remains of the two victims on December 31 after they had been eaten by lions. "Many more people may cross and get killed that we don't even know about," Mr. Pretorius said. "I got there at 12 pm and there was very little of them left. Another night and the hyenas would have eaten everything and there would have been no trace."

This had an immediate effect and they scattered as the grass caught fire.

It was fanned by the breeze into an instant blaze which quickly spread. The fire went for three days and fifty miles before dying out. The lions disappeared, not to be seen again. The fire probably drove out the poachers also.

Bob Cronchey, ex-Kenyan rancher and Ker & Downey guide, was dozing in his Land Rover when a large male lion started to lick his elbow's salty sweat. He woke with a jolt. The lion casually walked away after urinating on his front wheel. Fred Bartlett was camping in northern Botswana on the Kwando River, where Bushmen would hang around in the vicinity to get meat. One morning some Bushmen came over carrying an old man with a wounded leg. He had been sleeping next to a campfire when a lion crept up, grabbed his leg, and dragged him off. When he cried out, his wife woke and hurled a burning coal at the lion. It released the Bushman and ran off. A month later, at another camp on the Kwando River, a lioness killed a Bushman, dragged him off, and started to eat him. The camp staff alerted a professional hunter, Bert Milne, who drove out, saw it in his headlights, and killed it. Fred Bartlett always liked to use a white mosquito net while in lion country. He thought the lion could scent a human under the net but could not be sure whether the human was awake or asleep. Fred believes that a lion does not like to attack an object it cannot see clearly. I am sure there is truth in this, after all, all sorts of animals are stampeded into corrals with just plastic sheets. The frightened animals perceived them as man-made and barriers.

One morning, in Camp Saiele, I got up and walked around while brushing my teeth. After a few paces I noticed fresh lion spoor, and from the tracks saw where a male lion had walked right up to where I had been sleeping. After walking around the tent, it left. Some might conclude the lion had already eaten and was not hungry. I discovered later, following the tracks, that there were three lions — one male and two lionesses. One possibility is that my tent reeked of oil paint and turpentine, something that could deter anything. A Cape buffalo painting was one of the results of that trip. Early the next year, Fred Bartlett and his nephew Mike were in my own studio and helped me with their criticism. It was neat to have such experts guide me on such an important painting.

In June 1996, an American banker played a round of golf at Victoria Falls' Elephant Hills golf course alone. At the conclusion of 18 holes, during which he encountered no other golfers, he was met by a crowd of about two dozen spectators who applauded him as he putted out the final green. Bemused, he asked: "Why the accolades? Why the spectators?" They responded: "Didn't you see the sign on the first tee? It discouraged golf today because a lioness and her cubs were prowling the course." The banker continues to dine out on the story.

While on safari with Jack Nicklaus a few years ago we had occasion to play golf at the Leopard Creek Golf Club where Jack's home overlooks the Crocodile river onto the beautiful Kruger National Park. One afternoon we went fishing but were advised not to travel alone and to be in by dusk. Apparently lions and leopards are not at all uncommon on the property. When I asked Jack how they handle that type of hazard, he very coolly replied: "We step aside and let them play through."

AGGRESSIVE LIONS

There are many different attitudes that lions can have, and indeed, that any one lion can have. One that most seem to have is curiosity. When lions are curious, they approach and, as an artist I find it very easy to interpret this behavior as aggressiveness.

Chris McBride has walked thousands of miles photographing African wildlife and lions. While in Timbavatti, a nature reserve in the Republic of South Africa, he was looking for some of their white lions. One night he was sleeping in the back of a pickup truck with two friends.

At about two in the morning, Mandaban started to nudge me and whisper urgently in my ear. I woke up to find that the lions were all around us. There were three white lions in the Timbavatti pride and they were right on top of us. It was a bright, moonlit night and we could see their heads, which were higher than the level at which we had been sleeping. Instantly my instinct was to remain as quiet as possible and not to do anything. But as the minutes ticked away, the situation became more and more terrifying. They were so close. If one of them had taken it into his head to leap aboard to investigate, we'd have been finished. Lying down, as we were, in the back of the open pickup, we were completely defenseless. In the past I had always found that if I stood up suddenly in a situation like this, the lions would slink away immediately, just as they normally do when you approach them on foot. I decided that the safest thing would be to do just this. Then, as soon as they withdrew, we'd leap out of the back of the truck and run round to the cab. Inside the cab, at least we would have some protection. I whispered to the others to be ready to make a run for the cab and then stood up, making quite a noise in the process.

The lions had fled except for one, who began to make a mock charge that landed him six paces from the truck. This was a moment to stand firm and exude confidence and force the lion to back away. The trouble was that on this occasion I had only a small rifle with me, and there was no way it would have stopped that lion if he ever started to spring. I knew that, and I suppose he sensed something in my fear. What seemed like hours I stood there, the inadequate rifle cocked and pointed at him, the animal crouched in the position lions always adopt

prior to a spring—front paws stretched out, head low on the ground, hind quarters slightly raised, I didn't know for sure whether he was going to spring or not, but I couldn't afford to take the chance. If he had come at us, there was no chance at all that the rifle could have stopped him in mid-air. He would have landed right in the back of the pickup and would have taken at least one of us with him. So I fired.

Fortunately his shot, though of small caliber, dropped the lion, which died later. Chris was sorry for killing it, but I'll bet his two friends weren't.

Game-lodge manager and ex-hunter Douglas Collins has had many experiences with lions and advises, "As with all dangerous game, one cannot be dogmatic about summing them up. However, when confronted by any lion, always remember to put on a bold front, for he will sense timidity or fear in a human immediately." There have been hundreds of man-lion encounters in which lions ignored their terrified human acquaintances. The Owenses had many such hair-raising incidents. In one of them, Mark was driving away from camp one evening when two huge male lions framed the entrance to Delia's tent. Their heads were above her toes. When they smelled the tent floor their whiskers actually brushed against her sleeping bag. Hoping to attract Mark, she turned her flashlight on and off. This didn't disturb the lions at all, but it did cause Mark to return. When he arrived at her tent the lions were finally persuaded by his banging on the truck to move away, however reluctantly. This occurred, if you can imagine, just after they heard about a woman being dragged from her sleeping bag by lions in Chobe, a park in northeast Botswana. When you consider the many close Kalahari encounters that the Owenses had that did not end in tragedy, it makes one wonder.

In another incident that occured while doing her fieldwork, Delia Owens had a pair of lions stick their heads right into her tent with their whiskers actually brushing her ankles! Delia told me

The Sunday Times
August 4, 1985

KRUGER ANIMALS PREY ON FLEEING BLACKS

Thousands of Mozambican refugees — some falling prey to lions and other wild animals — have fled through the Kruger Park into South Africa. The refugees are so desperate to get into South Africa that they brave the wild animals in the Kruger Park and at least two Mozambicans have been killed in recent months. Mr. Kloppers said, "It is difficult to tell how many have been killed, because we only come across the bodies by chance."

that in the two decades of their work in Africa, they encountered only one human fatality by a lion:

Lions in remote areas or in national parks that have not had negative encounters with people do not seem to be nearly as dangerous to man as those that have. Admittedly, however, as specialists in animal behavior, we learned how to "read" lions very well, and could tell when and how to avoid dangerous situations. By the way, most of the dangerous encounters we had with lions involved our attempting to immobilize them with a capture rifle. For several years we did not even own a firearm while in the Kalahari. It was Phil Parkin, a Safari South hunting client, who kindly gave us his rifle for protection. In more than two decades of working in close proximity with wild animals — including "dangerous carnivores" — in Africa, we never fired a shot.

I was in that same area of the Chobe River in the late 1970s. A lion had dragged the assistant cook out of a tent at Camp Saiele. The cook ran after the lion and his terrified victim, banging two large pans on the cat's back. The lion dropped the poor man, who was actually back at work the next day with one very sore rear end and a heavily bandaged foot. When I mentioned to the camp manager how brave and plucky I thought the cook was, he laughed. I was informed that the cook simply did not want to do all the cooking himself, nor lose his authority over another worker!

The Owenses had many unusual, close encounters with lions. They were fortunate. Their very perceptive experiences and their ability not to panic let them appreciate these occurrences. Just look at the photo in *Cry of the Kalahari* of Mark sitting with Bimbo, a young male lion. Bimbo's face is about twenty inches from Mark. Apparently, the lions they worked near had become so accustomed to the Owenses that they were accepting them in a very unusual manner. Their ability to read the many moods of lions is nothing short of miraculous. They enjoyed the close presence of wild lions far more intimately than did anyone else I know. I shudder, however, at how many other people "in tune with nature" have not read their relationships with dangerous animals as well, or were as lucky as the Owenses.

I can't help thinking of an enthusiastic young man in Alaska. When warned about the danger of bears on the creek to which he was heading, he shrugged his shoulders and said "...if you don't bother them they won't bother you." His shredded knapsack was found a few weeks later along with one of his shoes. His foot was still in the shoe. Alaskan outfitter Keith Johnson flew me to many areas showing me many grizzlies. One of the biggest was in that same creek where the unfortunate individual was last seen alive.

Most lions want nothing to do with man if they have a choice. I used to think that all wild animals had a natural, instinctive, hereditary fear of man, but the Owenses have a very different point of view.

In remote areas where wild animals have not been exposed to man, they can be very naive and delightfully unafraid of humans. We have had the joy of walking along the deserted beaches of some of the remote islands that can only be reached by sailing for days. Wild birds such as fairy terns and frigates fly right up to your face and flutter around your head as they look you curiously in the eyes. You can sit cross-legged next to chicks on the beach and watch as their mothers bring them food. Giant sea turtles behaved the same way. And our experience in the Kalahari was filled with such encounters with animals, which did not know man, and were thus unafraid of us. We had mongooses on our bed, ratels in our cereal, hornbills on our

heads, lions in our kitchen boma, *hyenas in our bath* boma, *jackals in our dining tent, and on and on. It is certainly true that most wild animals fear us, but the degree to which this is instinctive is wide open to debate. Most animals have learned their fear of man — with good reason — and mothers pass it on to their young, from generation to genera-tion. Wild lions that we knew from birth, and those whom we knew had never seen other humans, seemed completely relaxed around us, to such an extent that we could walk among them to collect their scats while they were resting during the day. On a num-ber of occasions, cubs whose mother we had immobilized, wandered around us, curiously staring at us as we worked with their "sleep-ing" mother. We had similar experiences with leopards.*

The lion that has lived around man, however, knows that we are the only creature that can kill from afar, and they fear us as much as most of us fear deadly snakes. John Taylor, one of the legends of African hunting who spent most of his adult life in the bush, thought that the ordinary lion would never attack man unless provoked into doing so. George Schaller agrees, but with a very important addition: "Yes, if you know all the reasons why he might be provoked. But you can't know if the lion is disquieted by something that happened yesterday or reminded of something in the past. He does not want to fight; he does not want trouble. He will leave you alone if you leave him alone. He does not like having to get out of your way, naturally, but he will do so rather than start a row. He simply does not want to have anything to do with man." Apart from wild dogs and hyenas, man is the lion's only real enemy. Although the experience may not be a particularly pleasant one, you may quite safely meet a lion face to face when you are unarmed. Provided that you do not do anything foolish or lose your

head, the chances are a hundred to one that he will not molest you, even if there are several of them; just hope you won't meet one on that one hundredth time. On too many occasions I've met lions in just such a manner when I had nothing more lethal on me than binoculars and a walking stick. You're supposed to just look at one another until his curiosity is appeased. You really don't have much choice anyway. To run would surely cause its predator instinct to attack you.

As I pointed out in the first part of this book, if a lion is not hunting it probably won't interfere with you; if it is hunting, you won't see it. But it of course depends on the lions encountered. Some observers apparently encounter very aggressive lions and others obviously meet more timid animals. Taylor says that once lions realize that it's a man he is looking at he will usually move off into the grass with a little grunt and give you the road. And later "will probably tell his pals about the encounter in exactly the same slightly-breathless manner in which you would tell yours." These, however, are words from a hunter whose encounters were in areas where lions had consistently been hunted and had cultivated a very healthy respect for what hunters are capable of doing. According to Heinrich Lichtenstein, the charge of a lion is easily checked—even without a gun. The German zoologist, who lived for some time in the Cape, quotes local farmers as saying that an unarmed man was in no danger if he stared a charging lion in the eye. "With perfect steadiness and composure... the lion is supposed to become con-fused, retreating slowly at first and then faster and faster... Hasty flight by the pursued person, on the other hand, was said invari-ably to induce the lion to take up the chase, the unfortunate person soon being overtaken and killed." Not to nitpick, but I wonder how we would hear of the unsuccessful people who tried, but were killed, when they resorted to not moving. Guggisberg describes what he heard from local farmers about facing lions. "The settler's advice was quite well founded... although standing absolutely motionless may not be a complete guarantee of safety, it is certainly much better than running away. On more than one occasion a charging lion has turned aside only a short distance from the hunter who did not move, to chase after one of his companions who

Neck N' Neck, Oil on Canvas

had lost his head and run away." One man who tried it was George Rushby, the East African government official who was responsible for getting rid of the Njombe man-eaters in Tanzania. In his incident the lion pulled up at fifteen paces, turned tail, and fled. J.H. Patterson also observed that a charging lion would stop and slink away if its intended victim stood still and stared. If you are in front of one of those lions that are the exception, however, such statistics don't mean a thing.

Game rangers rarely go about armed in African game reserves unless they are on control work, and usually a threatening gesture or shout is enough to send the lion loping off into the bush. The former warden of Kruger National Park, Colonel J. Stevenson-Hamilton, says, "Lions can be very troublesome animals, especially at night when they jump over my fence looking for livestock. They wreak havoc in my cabbage patch. I have to go there and wave my hat at them and say 'Shoo!' That scares them!" He obviously has only met more docile lions. Knowing them well is very important. There are many people killed by lions in that part of Africa, particularly since the political problems in Mozambique have been making refuges walk unarmed through major lion areas.

John Northcote is one of the great professional hunters of the old school. Like many "European" Africans, he has had a remarkable life. I have been fortunate to spend many safari days with John and men like him, and of course I have learned much. He told me of a lion visiting while he and a friend, Cole, were sleeping in a fly camp. It was a bright moonlit night, and something woke him. He saw a lioness walking by and shook Cole to warn him. Cole told him to go back to sleep; "She is only looking for a snack." The next morning two very shaken game scouts told them the camp warthog was gone. "Where did you put it?" asked Cole. "It was lying between us, where we thought it would be safe," was the reply. The lioness had carefully stepped over them and taken the warthog without waking them.

Charles Williams of the Friedkin Companies had a sniffing lion one foot from his face through only the mosquito netting. The cat completely ignored his flashlight and noise and unceremoniously turned to spray the tent and him as its territory. John Davey, who worked with Williams in Botswana, was eating brunch in the central Kalahari when a lion came up and took the cooked meat right off the table in front of the terrified clients. Can you even imagine?

In Lion Country Safari, in southern Georgia in July 1971, South African Barry Styles had a two-and-a-half-year-old, hand-raised male lion. Against all rules, a family went through the park with the car windows open. Their four-year-old daughter had her head and arms out the window when the lion leaped for the girl. He had the front half of his body fully inside the car, and pulled the terrified girl out through the window. The lion was standing over her, apparently not knowing what to do, when Barry came up from behind, clapped his hands, and chased the lion away. Miraculously, the child had only minor wounds.

On the Kiangini River in Kenya, German Doctor Rudolf Harth shot a leopard on a bait in a tree. Instead of leaping off the tree and disappearing into the bush, the wounded leopard was trying desperately to hang onto the limb. Harth shot it again and it fell. To his astonishment, a lion, which was hidden under the tree, grabbed the leopard and ran off with it in his mouth.

Ettore Mocci and Hugo Seia were in Zambia in the summer of 1985. They were in a grass blind when they saw a young male lion appear. It came toward them and was just under the blind. He stood for a while, then decided to take a look from behind. Without breathing, Mocci says, "We waited until we saw the tip of its nose on Hugo's side. Hugo suddenly shook the flimsy blind with its dry leaves making quite a noise. I will never forget the noise, the fear, and the speed of that young lion rushing back towards the bait and then, just as fast, he rushed into thick grass."

On August 18, 1997, a pride of lions had to be killed in Kruger National Park because they ate some illegal immigrants from Mozambique. The immigrants use Kruger National Park as an access route and sometimes lions eat them. This was the fourth such incident by the same pride. According to Pascal Parent, it happened in the Pafuri area near Punda Maria, a water point used by a pride of lions. This pride learned that a human is an easy catch, and had therefore become man-eaters.

Nothing Unnoticed, Oil on Canvas

When I was on safari in Zambia in 1972, my guide and I were walking through some relatively safe, short grass, or so we thought. A lioness stood up in front of us, giving a very menacing growl. In an instant all hell broke loose, and there were lions everywhere. We froze, then slowly began to back off. At first this seemed to encourage more threats. We kept our eyes on the cats, backed oh-so-slowly away, and were eventually able to leave. It was absolutely terrifying. We concluded they were not hungry, but that we had interrupted their siesta.

Not all camp visits by lions end with the lion departing peacefully. Robin Hurt tells of a friend of his in Botswana, sleeping in the open near her car in a sleeping bag, who had a very unpleasant experience.

The lion came into the camp quietly, grabbed hold of her sleeping bag, luckily by the feet end, and proceeded to drag her, inside the bag and between his legs, out of camp. She woke up in the midst of this thinking it was a bad dream. She soon realized it was not. Luckily she had the presence of mind to remain silent and not panic, and gradually managed to wriggle out of the sleeping bag. The lion did not seem to notice the difference in the drag weight, perhaps because the sleeping bag kept getting tangled in the bush, and he had to struggle to free it. Anyway, she made her escape, ran back to her car, woke up her friend, and quickly got into the car. Meanwhile in the direction of the now empty sleeping bag, all hell broke loose, when the lion found his tasty morsel had escaped. He came back and circled the car for the rest of the night! What a sleepless night, but a lucky escape."

Robin was fly-camping with Bilu Dean and Rick Hopcraft, at Murungu Springs in the Moyowosi of western Tanzania, when a big lion came into camp.

Bilu and Rick were sleeping fairly close together, and I was sleeping some fifty yards away, nearer to the staff. It was a quiet night, pitch black with no moon. I could hear the lion approaching for a long time and I could hear Rick snoring. The lion was getting closer and closer and I was enjoying listening to him. Rick was sound asleep but Bilu was not. Suddenly I heard a muted voice saying "Rick, can you hear that?" No reply. A few minutes later, the lion was really close and roaring to beat hell, with his voice reverberating through the forest and our camp. Slightly louder this time, I heard Bilu saying "Rick, wake up, do you hear that?" No reply from the oblivious Rick. Nothing! By now the lion was well and truly in the camp and I got out of bed and grabbed my rifle as he was obviously very close to where Rick and Bilu lay. All the staff woke up too. Somewhere under my bed I found a flashlight and ran towards Bilu and Rick. Bilu was now yelling at the top of his voice, "Rick, Rick, do you hear that?" Half-asleep Rick rolled over and said quite casually, "Bilu, it is only a lion!" Bilu's shouting almost immediately changed to a whisper, and he said, "Yes, Rick, I know it's a lion. It is by the foot of your bed." This got Rick's attention and he sat up and looked straight into the eyes of a huge maned lion, three or four feet away. By this time the staff and I had arrived on the scene, and with much commotion and bellowing, scared the lion off. We all laughed for hours afterwards, about how soundly Rick could sleep!

Two of Hurt's hunters, Johnny Yakas and Gordy Church, were opening roads in his Mlele concession in South Tanzania.

> *As we normally do, when we are road build-*
> *ing, the hunters and the safari staff were*
> *sleeping in the open on the ground around*
> *the camp fire. It had been a hard day's work*
> *and they were all in deep slumber. Little did*
> *they know that during the night they had*
> *had a ghostly visitor in the form of a large*
> *lion. In the morning, they woke up and*
> *Johnny noticed lion tracks right by his head!*
> *This alerted everybody very quickly and it*
> *was immediately apparent, from the tracks,*
> *that the lion had walked through the sleep-*
> *ing group and even stepped across the bodies*
> *of some individuals and went on his way*
> *without disturbing anybody. They were for-*
> *tunate. He could have killed any one of the*
> *group with ease.*

Brian Nicholson, the famous Selous warden, who was on a foot safari with porters had an almost identical situation occur, but with a tragic difference. In this case the lion grabbed hold of one of his sleeping porters by his head, and dragged him soundlessly out of camp. No one woke up. In the morning they got up and became aware that one of the group was missing. Lion tracks were every-where, and it was evident that something terrible had happened. Brian straight away followed the drag mark and found the lion still on his grisly kill, and shot him dead. He says:

> *The moral of these stories is, when you hear a*
> *lion roaring at night, you really don't have*
> *much to worry about; on the contrary, it is*
> *when you don't hear him, that you had better*
> *watch out!*

James Robertson, another Kenyan guide, was camping in the Samburu area one evening when several lionesses visited the camp with their young cubs. The cubs apparently had a ball, with all the new toys to play with. They raised hell all night long while the staff were terrified. About the turn of the last century, Rachel Stuart Watt chased away two lions with a blast from her whistle. In her book, Jan Hemsing tells us of Kenyan columnist Edward Rodwell's safari when they stopped to camp for the evening. A small boy leading a herd of goats came into view. The boy greeted them and led the goats to the top of a small hill. Just before dark they could see him sitting among the animals. When darkness fell, they heard the bleating of the goats and the thin, reedy sound of a pipe. At about midnight they were awakened by lions; their roars came from the direction of the river. They seemed to be calling one another. The lions approached the camp. When one seemed to be a couple of hundred yards away, one of the men switched on the lorry's headlights. One lion roared very close to them. From the top of the hillock they heard the sound of the small boy's pipe; the thin, reedy tune scattered its notes among the surrounding bush. The boy played until the sounds of the lion died away. Then there was silence except for the cries of the night birds. They turned in again and slept soundly until dawn. Then they heard the goats and saw them scrambling down the hillside, the herdboy amongst them. They gave him bread and tea which he gratefully acknowl-edged. "Weren't you afraid of the lions?" Rodwell asked the boy. "No," he replied, "When I play my pipe the lions won't come near us." "With some feelings of shame I envied him his courage," Rodwell wrote. "He was such a small boy, and so far from home."

CAPTIVE LIONS

Lions in the wild are, under normal circumstances, reasonably predictable, intelligent, and shy. This is definitely not the case with lions in captivity. Captivity can often dull intelligence in an animal, and in lions it appears to have some fairly profound effects. They are fed regularly, so they no longer have to hunt. James Clark points out that circus lions, whether they are trained in the old way, with whips and chains, or with animal psychology or affec-tion training, are either passive, couldn't-give-a-damn lions, or mean and dangerous. About a hundred circus men have been killed while performing with lions, as have more zoo attendants.

Mbogo, Oil on Canvas

Lion tamer Hans Brick, whose animal-taming father was killed by a circus tiger, preferred to capture his recruits in the wild, for he found wild lions held man in respect as a "superior animal." Circus trainer Dick Chipperfield, too, frequently went to Africa to capture young lions for his circus. He and his family at one time owned more than five hundred lions. Chipperfield claimed that almost all tamers killed by lions were victims of male lions. He very seldom had a male in the ring with a female. He thought that males were liable to mistake you for a rival and would not miss an opportunity to assert their superiority.

A common cause of death in the ring is the result of a trainer backing into an animal or treading on its tail or foot. In March 1932, Chipperfield saw his own brother-in-law, Captain Purchase, misjudge an action in a small cage in the ring and confuse a male lion. The lion sprang at him and began to tear at him as he lay helpless in the sawdust. Chipperfield slipped into the cage as the audience began to scream hysterically, and attacked the lion with a feeding fork. He got the fork into the lion's mouth and began to jab it into his throat. Purchase was dragged out by attendants, but died three weeks later from infection.

Infection was responsible for several deaths in circuses in the early days, and quite often a clawing from a lion could carry such potent bacteria that it was comparable to being bitten by a venomous snake. Chipperfield himself might have died many times had it not been for antibiotics.

Lionesses apparently accept trainers as a male lion. Clark has seen them take the side of a trainer who is threatened by a male lion. That is exactly what happened to Josip Marcan, the lion trainer in Deland, Florida. Josip told me that one of his largest lionesses seemed to be imprinted on him, and would always defend him from any other lion that might get nasty with him. His life was actually saved twice by this animal. On one of those occasions the "nasty" lion was already on top of him, with Marcan's arm in its mouth.

Harold Davidson gave up the cloth to become a showman. One day, in Pleasureland, Skegness, England, Davidson stood on a lioness's tail. As his horrified audience looked on, the lioness clawed him to the ground and then carried him in her mouth to a corner, where she killed him. Sometimes captive lions that go berserk attempt to eat their victims.

Hans Brick once had a most seemingly cooperative lion which he captured himself in West Africa. Within a short time of its capture, though, the animal consumed a groom, who, coming home drunk, had staggered against the bars. "He was killed and devoured through the cage bars," says Brick. Only a few pieces of cloth and a shoe were recovered.

In 1966, a show lion escaped near Kampala, Uganda, and killed seven people before it was shot. In odd places, circus and zoo lions have escaped from time to time, but rarely with such disastrous results. Usually, after a trained lion escapes, it seeks a place to hide. Guggisberg gives an excellent example of this. Someone telephoned Dr. Gebbing, former director of the Leipzig Zoo, to say that an escaped circus lion was sitting on the roof of a building. Gebbing advised them to get its cage and put it near the lion and then move in on the lion. It will seek the safety of its own cage, the doctor assured them. That is precisely what happened.

In October, 1996, a lioness escaped from a travelling circus in the Chilean town of El Melon, and took a nap in a terrified family's bedroom, the child in the bedroom said. The lioness was awakened and captured by her keepers with the help of Chilean police. Her keepers had forgotten to close the door to her cage after retrieving some lion cubs. "I told my mother it was a lion, but she refused to believe me until she saw the animal lying on the bed."

Michael Dee, Curator of Mammals at the Los Angeles Zoo, told me of an incident when he was senior keeper in 1980. One afternoon in October, the remains of a man with a large crucifix was found in a lion cage. Mike had the grisly task of dragging out the remains. "It appeared that he had climbed the bottlebrush tree and was attempting to lower himself into the exhibit when the male lion jumped up and grabbed him by the throat and dropped him in the stairwell." Because the bottom of the stairwell was not in the public's line of sight, Mike told me, the lion, whose name was Pookie, had a few hours in which he ate about forty pounds of the unfortunate fellow. "For the next week, Pookie had loose stools, and finally passed all of the hand bones and a portion of the vic-

The Natal Witness

December 29, 1992

THE KING OF THE BEASTS CAN OPEN CAR DOORS — CLAIM

A lion at a local game park has learned how to open car doors, claims Lorna McConnel, a recent visitor to the park. McConnel says that, as she and her group were driving through the lion enclosure at the Lion's Park near Cato Ridge on Saturday, a lion went up to the car in the front of them and opened the door with its mouth. She said that before the animal could attack the occupants, the girl in the back seat slammed the door shut and then locked it. The lion then went around to the other door and attempted to open it.

tim's T-shirt that had been eaten." The man apparently thought he was Daniel and could walk with the lions. Jeanne Minor of the National Zoo in Washington, D.C., told me of a distraught woman who jumped into the lion area and was killed and partially eaten in early 1995.

Mike Kinsey, retired Curator of Mammals for the Denver Zoo, was describing to me how different so many of the lion personalities were, but I must admit that the imagination and intelligence of one lioness stands out. "Holly" was nothing short of brilliant.

All the other lionesses tended toward the typical zoo-soft and pudgy big cats, but Holly stayed trim all her life. She was sleek, brilliant, and carried a disdain for our species that gave the word "aloof" a transcendent meaning. As a cub, she and her two other siblings could not jump up to the shelf to the transfer door. The other cubs would hiss and snarl at the zookeeper like any frightened, bluffing lion cub should. Holly would just follow him with her eyes everywhere he went, not missing a thing he did. One day he put a small log about a foot and a half in diameter into the cage for the adult lioness to use as a scratching device. The next day, to the keeper's astonishment, Holly blithely followed her mother into the transfer ramp. She had jumped onto the log and from there to the ramp. Thinking it a coincidence, the keeper emptied the cage, put the log in its far corner, and let the lions back in. Later he opened the transfer ramp and the mother went through. Still too small to jump the distance, Holly dragged and pushed the log from the far corner of the cage to where it was under the ramp entrance whereupon she leaped onto the log and then to the ramp.

The other two cubs never caught on to this and could not make it till they grew big enough to make it without using the log. When Holly was an adult her new keeper left a lock hanging unlocked in the securing hasp. It was, however, hanging closed and gravity kept it in place. Three tiger cubs were in that other connecting but closed cage. Holly was able to jiggle the lock out of the hasp and open the cage with tragic results. She killed two of the three tiger cubs. After that she checked every lock on every door on every day even to the point of flicking them with her paw or jiggling the doors if she suspected they were not secure. On another occasion an ad agency put a mannequin in the outdoor lion exhibit to photograph the lions inspecting their new clothing line. One lion ran to the corner, more startled than scared. The second was scared and never came out into the exhibit. Holly, however, immediately dropped to her belly in a typical lion stalking position. Her eyes widened and ears slowly laid back. Then, in two strong bounds, she cleared the forty feet to the model and, with a powerful roundhouse, beheaded the dummy. In no time the mannequin was destroyed. Then she leveled her chilling gaze on the people amassed out front.

I for one have no problem getting that message. In May, 1993, one Alfred Rials inexplicably scaled two fences and a building to land smack in the middle of the lions' outdoor African Plains exhibit at New York's Bronx Zoo. He spent ten minutes sitting between two lions, in front of some horrified spectators. The lions, just curious at first, quickly began slapping him around. Senior keeper Loraine Hershonik eventually enticed the pair of 350-pound lions

Serengeti Chase, Oil on Canvas

The Pretoria News
July 25, 1997
LIONS EAT TWO ILLEGAL IMMIGRANTS
PAFURI — Two illegal Mozambican immigrants were eaten by lions in the Kruger National Park this week, Pafuri police said yesterday. Inspector Samson Shabalala said all that was left of an unidentified man and woman was a small bone which was found about 30 km from Pafuri camp, in the northern most part of the park, on Wednesday morning, it was reported. Insp. Shabalala said the two were part of a group of four illegal immigrants attempting to cross into South Africa. Only one of them was able to escape by climbing a tree. The man described how he had heard the lions devour his companions but could not say how many lions were involved. All that was left to identify the two people was a woman's blouse and skirt, and a man's T-shirt, trousers and shoes. Police followed the bloodied pile of clothes and fresh lion tracks to a spot 50 m away where more bloodied clothes and a small bone were found. And hyenas had eaten what was left by the lions.

Victoria Falls Lilac Breasted Roller

away. Rials received nineteen stitches in his head and face, and was hospitalized for psychiatric evaluation.

LIONS AS PETS

We are suffering from a glut of lions, says Saul Kitchener of the Lincoln Park Zoo in Chicago. Ten years ago, lions were selling for $50. When safari parks started opening, the price jumped to about $250. Now, they're not worth anything. You can't even give a lion away. He advertised unsuccessfully as far away as England to find a "responsible institution" to take lions they no longer had room for at the zoo. Fortunately, families who want a pet lion aren't considered responsible institutions. African-style parks used to pounce eagerly on surplus zoo lions. Now the parks are overpopulated with lions as well.

Many people have tried to make pets of lions. As cubs they are delightful but difficult. At one year old, they're less fun and ten times the work. At two years old, they don't know their own incredible strength or their instinctive killing reflexes. Many an experienced lion trainer has found out the hard way what all inexperienced lion-pet keepers are doomed to learn: They are just plain dangerous. Professional hunter Lionel Hartley's mother, Diana Hartley, was killed by her own very affectionate pet lion. Used in the film *Hatari*, with John Wayne, the lion had been kept tied up by the producer of the film for a good while in Diana's absence. On her return, she ran to greet the tied-up lion, which was elated to see her. He jumped on her so enthusiastically that he killed her.

Joy and George Adamson of *Born Free* fame certainly had much experience with captive lions. Whether they learned from it or not is not very apparent. Television nature shows may make mild references to the fact that it is unwise to keep wild animals for pets; the truth is that it's just damned foolish. After George Adamson was killed in 1989 by one of his own pet lions, the three remaining lions were brought into Botswana from Kenya by Gareth Patterson. George was actually mauled three times by these various pets before the last one did it to finality. Furaha, one of the three lionesses, killed Isaac Mangogola, a game tracker. Although also reported to have been killed by one of their lion pets, his wife

Joy's death appears now to be a murder. The Adamsons' idea of putting pet lions back into the wild was costly and unscientifically sentimental. Money used to reintroduce the animals to the wild would have been better spent on research. Lions, once used to human contact, are a very great danger.

In his book *African Hunter,* Bror von Blixen-Finecke describes a pet lion, Kom, that was quite independent at the age of six weeks, and whose intelligence was more developed than that of a puppy the same age. At six months Kom was a fine big lion. An ox, which had broken its leg, was killed, and Kom was present at the execution. When the ox fell and the smell of blood came to the young lion, he was on the fallen animal in a single bound. He began to lap the oxen's blood and defended his catch with terrifying ferocity. When he had eaten his fill he slipped back into pet life as if nothing had happened. And they still kept it as a pet.

The great writer Beryl Markham was mauled when she was a child, by a neighbor's pet lion, Paddy. Beryl was one incredible woman. Her father alone raised her. She grew up with the Nandi *moran*, young warriors who would let her accompany them on their hunts. She learned to hunt with spear as well as gun. She was Kenya's first female horse trainer and first female bush pilot. Markham made headlines as the first person ever to fly westward over the Atlantic. She did it solo and she did it the hard way; against headwinds from east to west. I cannot recommend too highly her book *West with the Night*.

Her father warned her that "a domesticated lion is an unnatural lion — and whatever is unnatural is untrustworthy." I would like to quote this story from her book. On a walk to Elkington's, their neighbor in British East Africa (now Kenya) where she grew up, she describes meeting the lion, Paddy, alone on the road.

> *I remembered the rules that one remembers.*
> *I did not run. I walked very slowly, and I*
> *began to sing a defiant song. "Kali coma*
> *Simba sisi," I sang, "Asikari yoti ni udari! —*
> *Fierce like the lion are we, Askari all are*
> *brave!" I went in a straight line past Paddy,*
> *when I sang it, seeing his eyes shine in the*
> *thick grass, watching his tail beat time to the*

metre of my ditty. "Twendi, twendi — ku pigana — piga adoui — piga sana! — Let us go, let us go — to fight — beat down the enemy! Beat hard, beat hard!" What lion would be unimpressed with the marching song of the King's African rifles? Singing it still, I took up my trot toward the rim of the low hill, which might, if I were lucky, have Cape gooseberry bushes on its slopes. The country was gray-green and dry, and the sun lay on it closely, making the ground hot under my bare feet. There was no sound and no wind. Even Paddy made no sound, coming swiftly behind me.

What I remember most clearly of that moment that followed are three things—a scream that was barely a whisper, a blow that struck me to the ground, and as I buried my face in my arms and felt Paddy's teeth close on the flesh of my leg, a fantastically bobbing turban, that was Bishon Singh's turban, appear over the edge of the hill. I remained conscious, but I closed my eyes and tried not to be. It was not so much the pain as the sound. The sound of Paddy's roar in my ears will only be duplicated, I think, when the doors of hell slip their wobbly hinges, one day, and give voice and authenticity to the whole panorama of Dante's poetic nightmares. It was an immense roar that encompassed the world and dissolved me in it. I shut my eyes very tight and lay still under the weight of Paddy's paws.

Bishon Singh said afterward that he did nothing. He said he had remained by the hay shed for a few minutes after I ran past him, and then, for no explainable rea-

son, had begun to follow me. He admitted, though, that, a little while before, he had seen Paddy go in the direction I had taken.

The Sikh called for help, of course, when he saw the lion meant to attack, and a half-dozen of Elkington's syces had come running from the house. Along with them had come Jim Elkington with a rawhide whip. Jim Elkington, even without a rawhide whip, was very impressive. He was one of those enormous men whose girths alone seem to preclude any possibility of normal movement, much less of speed. But Jim had speed—not to be loosely compared with lightning, but rather like the speed of something spherical and smooth and relatively irresistible, like the cannon balls of the Napolenic Wars. Jim was, without question, a man of considerable courage, but in the case of my rescue from the lion, it was, I am told, his momentum rather than his bravery for which I must be forever grateful.

It happened like this—as Bishon Singh told it: "I am resting against the walls of the place where hay is kept and first the large lion and then you, Beru, pass me going toward the open field, and a thought comes to me that a lion and a young girl are strange company, so I follow, I follow to the place where the hill that goes up becomes the hill that goes down, and where it goes down deepest I see that you are running without much thought in your head and the lion is running behind you with many thoughts in its head, and I scream for everybody to come very fast.

The Pretoria News
October 11, 1983

MAN KILLED, ANOTHER MAULED IN GAME PARK

HECTORSPRUIT — A man was mauled to death after he and two companions scaled three fences to get into a lion park. Another was rescued from a "playful" lioness found sitting on top of him. He was taken to hospital bleeding and covered with cuts and scratches. The third man escaped the pride of eight lions and four cubs at the Marlothi park near Tenbosch siding. Shortly afterward a lioness was found on top of a dead man. More screams attracted rangers to another man pinned beneath a lioness. "It appears she had been playing 'cat and mouse' with him for some time and a large area was covered in blood and pieces of clothing," Mr. Roos said.

"Everybody comes very fast, but the large lion is faster than anybody, and he jumps on your back and I see you scream but I hear no scream. I only hear the lion, and I begin to run with everybody, and this includes Bwana Elkington, who is saying a great many words I do not know and is carrying a long kiboko which he holds in his hand and is meant for beating the large lion.

"Bwana Elkington goes past me the way a man with lighter legs and fewer inches around his stomach might go past me, and he is waving the long kiboko so that it whistles over all our heads like a very sharp wind, but when we get close to the lion it comes to my mind that that lion is not of the mood to accept a kiboko.

"He is standing with the front of himself on your back, Beru, and you are bleeding in three or five places, and he is roaring. I do not believe Bwana Elkington could have thought that the lion at that moment would consent to being beaten, because the lion was not looking the way he had ever looked before when it was necessary for him to be beaten. He was looking as if he did not wish to be disturbed by a kiboko, or the Bwana, or the syces, or Bishon Singh, and he was saying so in a very large voice.

"I believe that Bwana Elkington understood this voice when he was still more than several feet from the lion, and I believe that Bwana considered in his mind that it would be the best thing not to beat the lion just then, but the Bwana when he runs very fast is like the trunk of a great baobob tree rolling down a slope, and it seems that because of this it was not possible for him to explain the thought of his mind to the soles of his feet in a sufficient quickness of time to prevent him from rushing much closer to the lion than in his heart he wished to be.

"And it was this circumstance, as I am telling it," said Bishon Singh, "which in my considered opinion made it possible for you to be alive, Beru." "Bwana Elkington rushed at the lion then, Bishon Singh?"

"The lion, as of the contrary, rushed at Bwana Elkington," said Bishon Singh. "The lion deserted you for the Bwana, Beru. The lion was of the opinion that his master was not in any honest way deserving of a portion of what he, the lion, had accomplished in the matter of fresh meat through no effort by anybody except himself." Bishon Singh offered this extremely reasonable interpretation with impressive gravity, as if he were expounding the Case For the Lion to a chosen jury of Paddy's peers.

"Fresh meat..." I repeated dreamily, and crossed my fingers. "So then what happened?" The Sikh lifted his shoulders and let them drop again. "What could happen, Beru? The lion rushed for Bwana Elkington, who in his turn rushed from the lion, and in so rushing did not keep in his hand the long kiboko and it fell to the ground. Then with two free hands the Bwana was fortunately able to ascend a narby tree." "And you picked me up, Bishon Singh?"

He made a little dip with his massive turban. "I was happy with the duty of carrying you back to this very bed, Beru, and of advising your father, who had gone to observe some of Bwana Elkington's horses, that you had been moderately eaten by the large lion. Your father returned very fast, and Bwana Elkington some time later returned very fast, but the large lion has not returned at all."

It continues to surprise me as to what goes through people's minds. Having pet lions in Africa is hard enough to understand, but in today's developed cities? Late in 1987, a man walked into a crowded, north Houston, Texas, shopping center with a full-grown lion tethered to a chain. The lion knocked something over and became excited. A little girl walked by, and he grabbed her by the head and started dragging her across the floor. She was screaming and all hell broke loose. A security guard shot the animal but authorities had trouble subduing the lion even after it was shot. One customer's understated response was, "You surely can't walk lions through a shopping center on a chain." Nine years earlier, in October 1978, twenty-six-year-old Margaret Haynie was killed by her husband's "very tame" pet lioness near Tallahassee, Florida.

Norman Carr raised two lions (Big Boy and Little Boy) in Zambia, from 1957 to 1962. (His son Adrian was the hunter who killed the lion that dragged professional hunter Peter Hankin from his tent and ate him.) Carr fed the lions with carcasses of normal lion prey, and being lions, they gorged themselves with enough food to easily last a few days. Norman's lions quite often wandered from the remote areas where he raised them. On one occasion they crossed the Nkala River into Kafue National Park for a few days. They hadn't quite learned to hunt for themselves and after awhile in the park, they probably got lonely for Norman, for when they saw a Land Rover coming down the park road they joyously raced over to the familiar-sounding vehicle. "Unfortunately for both parties it was not my Land Rover," said Carr. An Englishman on his first safari was driving alone on the park road looking for game when he saw the two lions running towards him. "He had expected to see lions, but he was not prepared for this," says Carr. The driver tried backing up but got stuck in the sand as one lion jumped on the hood and the other on top of the canvas top. "The canvas did not stand up to three hundred pounds of lion, so Big Boy sank through the roof onto the terrified man's lap." Can you even imagine? "Fear and desperation gave him strength enough to grab the lion by the mane and prevent the deadly fangs sinking into his throat. The fact that his assailant only wanted to lick him was lost on the frantic man. During the struggle, the door of the vehicle flew open and lion and man landed in a heap on the road. He

rushed around the back of the Land Rover with the intention of getting in through the other door, but on the other side he came face to face with Little Boy." The Englishman succeeded in getting into the vehicle and starting the engine, all the while being licked by Little Boy! He shot out of the sand and arrived back at camp trembling all over. He mentions that his liquor bill rose dramatically that day.

Carr's lions needed to be trained to hunt. In the course of four years, Big Boy and Little Boy were not nearly as ready as his friend Erica Critchley's pet leopard, which he trained to return to the wild in only four days.

LIONS GUARDING PROPERTY

Yes, you read it right. Lions are now being sold as guards. In Rio de Janeiro, Saldadino de Suza Gonzalez says he has the perfect solution for Brazilians wanting to protect their homes from burglars: guard lions. "With a lion for a guard, the thief may enter but he won't leave," said Gonzalez, a 45-year-old from Belo Horizonte, Brazil. Gonzalez has raised lions on his farm for ten years. Brazil's soaring crime rate has helped create a steady demand for them. "I recommend a large back yard, the construction of a gate, and plenty of space. Then let them roam free at night," Gonzalez said. Three lions guard Gonzalez's home. Gonzalez started with three lions smuggled from Africa, and now raises a litter every three months. When the cubs are thirty days old, he puts them up for sale for $300, using classified ads. Business is brisk. "Thieves are smart. They always scope out their targets. If there's a lion on the premises they won't try robbing the house," he said.

In April, 1993, lions mauled to death a thief who broke into a zoo in Namibia to steal mangoes. The lions were let out of their enclosure at night to deter would-be thieves from crossing perimeter fences, said Joe Bradley, a keeper at Ekongoro Zoo. When officials opened the zoo the next morning, the lions were sitting next to the corpse of twenty-year-old Lucas Tileni. Tileni crossed a twelve-foot double fence and a ditch to get into the zoo. Bradley said he raised the lions from cubs and they were "tame as pet dogs."

Lawyers and Bankers, Oil on Canvas

OPEN VEHICLES

In Africa, there is a firm belief among tourists and even some professional hunters that lions won't attack a person in a car. This belief has grown up largely with the advent of game reserves, in which people can safely drive up to big game in their vehicles. In most of these parks, lions tend either to ignore cars completely or to use them as a means of getting shade or ambushing antelope. Exhaust fumes mask human scent and the cab breaks up a person's recognizable human shape, but as always, when near lions, one is never completely safe.

Cincinnati Zoo director Ed Maruska told me of a time when he was in the Ngorongoro Crater with former Serengeti Game Warden Gordon Harve. Maruska was sitting on the roof of his vehicle watching a mating pair of lions. All at once, the male leaped up at him and, were it not for Gordon's quick action of pulling him down inside the vehicle, the Cincinnati Zoo might have had a new director.

Brian Herne, in Uganda, had a very angry lioness go for his Land Rover. She wound up on the hood, with her face a foot from his and only the windshield separating them. I used to drive in lion country with the windshield down.

In March 1962, Frederick van Wyk and Ronald Holloway were attacked as they slept in their car, half a mile south of the Chirundi Bridge over the Zambezi, between Kariba Dam and their hometown, Lusaka. They were severely mauled as they fought the lion inside the car. They finally managed to slam the door on its body, causing it to retreat.

The incident is not unique. James Clark tells of T. Murray-Smith arriving with the Maharajah of Jodphur in an open truck near Lake Manyara, Tanzania. A lion sprang onto the hood and smashed the windshield. The Maharajah shot it through the brain at a range of twelve inches. Douggie Wright, a professional hunter, had a charging lion come for the vehicle, and as the lion leaped, Wright fired. The lion crashed through the windshield, dying with a final shot on the front seat.

Soren Lindstrom is a huge fellow by any standards. He looks like a classic rugby player. Although I had known about him for years, I first met Soren in Maun, Botswana, in the mid 1990s. One story he told me was also described in *Hunting the African Lion,* an anthology edited by Jim Rikhoff. In it Lindstrom and some friends were photographing animals and hoped to get pictures of lions. He drove into some long grass where they had seen a magnificent lion. *"Look out! He's coming!"* was heard from the back of the Land Cruiser. As he turned to look back, to his horror he felt the vehicle rock as he saw a big lion spring at the occupants in the back. Lindstrom says, "With giant paws flailing and teeth bared, the roaring lion chose Mary as his target. She flung herself to the floor as the lion hit the metal bar surrounding the back of the truck, her only protection, and I drove off at full speed to get away from the beast." At that point he wanted to leave, but decided to go back just in case the lion might have been wounded. "If he charges, shoot him!" he told one of the hunters in the Land Cruiser, fearing that a wounded lion would raise hell, especially with any unarmed passersby. The lion charged again and was shot by the hunter, then ran for the closest bushes. Lindstrom left the scene, found a safe place for Mary and her family about a half-mile away, and went back for the probably wounded lion. Following the blood spoor past a fallen mopane tree, they went into thick grass, which was growing up among the dead mopane branches.

As I turned, I heard the growl, and the huge yellow ball of fury came right at me. "Why me?" I recall thinking. I swung around and fired at him as he sprang at me. I remember seeing stars as he hit—those ugly, beady eyes fixed on my throat and head.

Tiku climbed the nearest tree in great haste and Joseph dived into the nearest bush. Kirk sat in the car, horrified. The lion hit me so hard, with his jaws clamped around my upper arm, that I sailed through the air, firmly gripped by his huge, ugly yellow teeth. His mane hairs and my blood were later seen ten feet up in the clump of slim mopane trees immediately behind where I had stood. As we hit the ground, the lion shook me like a terrier shakes a rat.

Natal Observer
December 17, 1985

RANGERS KILL TWO LIONS
BUT HUNT GOES ON
Natal Parks Board rangers have killed a lion and a lioness believed to belong to the pride that devoured a game guard in the Hluhluwe Game Reserve. L-Cpl. Hlabisa was killed after he was thrown among the lions by his horse after he and another mounted guard had galloped into the pride while fleeing charging white rhino.

Lindstrom used almost the same words as David Livingstone in his lion incident recounted later on page 120.

I felt my arm snap and heard the horrific noise of breaking bones and tearing flesh. I felt no pain, just a strong will to survive and anger at this brute that was tearing me apart. For a moment, as my arm broke, the lion relaxed, probably thinking it was my neck! He lay on top of me possessively, I should have kept still, but instead, I threw my left arm over his neck, grabbed mane and ear and rolled him off me. Superhuman strength, the will to survive and, I guess, as a hunter, the fact that one has been beaten at one's own game came to mind as I fought against all odds the six-hundred-pound king of beasts. His powerful jaws once again took hold of my left upper arm, as I quickly moved it to protect my throat. Again he lifted me and shook me like a rag doll and dragged me off between his forelegs towards the bush where Joseph lay hoping he would not be seen.

For some reason Joseph got up and ran for his life, but he did not get far. The lion dropped me and pursued the new target. He took Joseph by the leg and bowled him over, and his jaws closed on the arm, which Joseph threw up to protect the vital neck and head. The lion hit so hard and fast that Joseph was knocked unconscious—fortunately for him. The lion lay on top of him possessively. At this point, I arose, I glanced at my arm, which I thought had been severed, but all I could see was mangled flesh and bare bones at the elbow joint and a fountain of blood spurting from a severed artery. Well aware of my serious condition, I immediately looked for my rifle, which I knew still held an unfired round. I realized that I had to shoot that lion before it killed Joseph—or was he already dead? I wasn't sure. I found the rifle and backed up against a tree, trying with my now-also-mangled left arm to get the rifle to my shoulder, but no way. Both my shoulders were dislocated from the violent shaking. I was helpless, but my legs worked, so I walked to the car—well aware of the lion, growling and snarling at me as I went. As I got into the car, I said to Kirk, "Take my belt off, and tie it tightly around my upper arm to arrest the bleeding from the severed artery." He was still in a state of horror, but as I spoke, he came to and reacted immediately. "Now drive the car at that lion, and chase it off Joseph." Kirk took over and reacted with a new sense of responsibility. Between he and Tiku—who now came down from the tree—they lifted Joseph into the back of the car, and Kirk drove off. Again the lion came out in hot pursuit of the vehicle. "My God, he's really cross," I tried to joke. "Make a big detour before you drive to where your Mom and the others are." We had a six-hour drive to the nearest airstrip, and I knew I could not make that drive. We had to get an aircraft and a doctor to land nearby. There was an open plain close by, and Kirk, who had some flying experience, ascertained that an aircraft could bank and take off. The radio was put up, and Kirk called "May Day." Mary and Sissy took over caring for Joseph and me.

We were both in bad shape, and the pain was becoming unbearable; I knew I was dying from loss of blood. The two ladies took

The Star

August 30, 1984

GERMAN GIRL (18) EATEN BY LIONESSES

MAUN (Botswana) — A German girl (18) has been killed and eaten by two lionesses in the Okavango Swamps. The girl was believed to have been part of a group of 30 German church youths who were camping in tents at Xaxanaka near Chief's Island in the middle of the wildlife sanctuary. Residents said the young people were sleeping in a tent which was not properly closed. At about 5 am yesterday a lioness dragged the girl out of her tent to a nearby ditch, where she was eaten. Attempts were made by the group to scare away the lioness who was joined by another after the girl was dragged from the tent. Botswana game scouts are believed to be hunting the lionesses.

turns gripping the severed artery, but the tourniquet, however tight, did not stop the gushing blood. I hoped that I would pass out, but I also realized that if I were to survive, I would have to stay with the program. Within three hours, two planes were alongside our car. One was flown by my good friend, Tim Liversedge, and the other by Tony Weeks, who had a doctor on board, as well as professional hunter Douggie Wright. Douggie took the LaVigne family back to the camp, and Joseph and I were flown to Maun. I woke up later that night in the Johannesburg General Hospital, where I was to spend the next three months. Joseph was released after six weeks from Maun Hospital. Nine months later I was back in the bush with clients—hunting again with the LaVigne family—and daily life as a professional hunter has continued. My right arm is fused at the elbow joint, and the bicep was totally removed. The lion did not know that I am left handed.

A few years later, at a charity dinner in Toronto with hunters Rose and Joe Wells, I had an interesting chat with the fellow sitting next to me. We exchanged some outdoor stories. He introduced himself as Warren Winkler, a sitting judge on the Ontario Supreme Court. As we talked, it came out that he had been the one who killed the huge "Lindstrom Lion" while hunting with Harry Selby in the Okavango in the fall of 1985. The world keeps getting smaller.

HUNTING LIONS WITH SPEARS

Before the days of colonialism, the Masai pursued their women- and cattle-rustling activities all across their world with no real constraints from their neighbors. They were the toughest of some very tough tribes. They are *the* lion hunters among many lion-hunting tribes. Their now-illegal ceremony of spearing a lion is well known. The Masai would provoke a lion into charging a youth who was then supposed to demonstrate his worth in order to be classed as a *moran*. These are the young warriors of the tribe, called *morani*. They subsist mainly on a diet of fresh blood and milk. The Nandi were another similar warlike people who occasionally attacked the Masai when high on native beer called *pombe*.

As the lion sprang, the youth would plant his spear with the butt firmly in the ground and point uppermost, then guide it so that the lion impaled itself. Later the ceremony became one of communally spearing the lion, and the man who first pulled its tail would get the honors. Several men would occasionally die in the attack or later from the infected wounds.

The story of lion spearing has been recorded in bronze. For years, there were two magnificent bronze sculptures of two Nandi spearmen and a pair of lions positioned in the main entrance to the American Museum of Natural History in New York. The spearmen were on the left and about thirty yards to the right were the lions. Unfortunately, because of the current dinosaur craze, they have been replaced by a Jurassic exhibit.

The Acholi tribesmen, living in the north near the Nile, are very brave and are good hunters and trackers. Buffalo are one of their main prizes. Buffalo provide lots of meat and lots of excitement. A group of fifteen to twenty men get themselves psyched up and go on a rampage, usually in a national park, where game is plentiful. They each carry spears about nine feet long, very sturdy, with two feet of steel at each end. They approach a herd of buffalo or a single bull and incite an animal to charge. The buffalo invariably singles out one man and goes for him. This man holds his ground while the others scatter and then come in from the side and behind. The man plants his spear in the ground, pointing it at the chest of the charging animal, as the Masai do with a lion. At the last second, a moment before impact, he jumps to one side as the bull, in full momentum, impales itself on the spear. The other tribesmen then come in and finish what the first plunging spear started to do. It does not always go that way however.

Victoria Falls Lion, Oil on Canvas

TRACKING

Those who have had the privilege of seeing an African tracker at work have witnessed one of the really remarkable talents of man. It's easy to understand how one can follow tracks in mud where there is no vegetation and the prints are very bold and easy to see. But when tracking leads over hard rock through tall grass, or across a desert of hot stones, it is simply beyond my comprehension how trackers do it. Read J.A. Hunter's description from his book *Hunter*:

> The tracks we were following were the freshest, although it is not always easy to tell the age of a track. Old pugmarks made in the lee of a bunch of grass and sheltered from the wind will often seem fresher than new tracks made in the open and full of drifted sand. Generally, old marks are covered by the tracks of small animals that have run over them, but the only sure way to tell that you are on a fresh spoor is to find some of the lion's droppings. A good tracker can tell at once from the condition of the droppings how long it is since the animal passed. The morani *were excellent at spooring. Often they would lift the branches of some low bush with their spears to show me marks that I would have missed. I noticed they did not go from pugmark to pugmark but seemed to follow the trail ten or fifteen paces ahead of them. They knew the habits of lions so perfectly they could roughly tell where the animals were likely to go. When at fault, they would stop and cast around, much like a pack of hounds that have lost the scent, examining every sandy spot nearby that might bear the impression of a pugmark until they had picked up the trail again.*

J.A. Jordan was amazed at their tracking prowess:

> Where I could see nothing they (Mongorrori trackers) padded on confidently as if following a road. Now and then even they had to halt, to prod among the pebbles and grass, their backs bent, their thin black legs stuck this way and that, until one would cry in high triumph, and off we went again. They read the trail plainly, in a scratch on the rocks, a breath of dust over a pebble, a half-bent grass-blade.

I spend a great deal of time in the field and have an excellent sense of direction, but it is nothing when compared to these fellows. After concentrating on the tracking for hours, zigzagging for miles on a gray day with no sun to guide by, in flat areas where there are no mountains or any other prominent landmarks, I would be completely disoriented. More than once have I thought the trackers dead wrong to not follow our tracks back to camp or our vehicle. But somehow, in a straight line, they would lead us back! These hardy men of the bush must have some extraordinary extrasensory directional ability.

Though lions can't be seen in the tall grass or thick bush, they are often located by the action of birds, which are very noisy in the presence of predators. Lilac-breasted rollers and fiscal shrikes in particular will gladly let you know that some kind of predator is just out of your sight. Here is a description from professional hunter Derek Dunn:

> A really first-class tracker can tell you the color of the mane in almost total desert country, where trees of any description are a rarity. With trackers like these you will follow the lion until sooner or later the lion, during the course of his travels, will lie down to rest. It is in such a place that the tracker will kneel close to the ground and spit all over the palm of his hand. Once the palm is moist he will gently dab his hand over the marks the lion has left during his siesta. Any strands of mane attach themselves to the tracker's palm. He pulls the hairs off his palm and deadpan will say blonde, or black, or red, or salt and pepper. 'That is the color of the mane, Bwana.'

The Citizen/Pretoria News
April 24, 1997

ATTACKED BY LION

SINGWEDZI — A Kruger National Park game ranger is in stable condition in Pshilidzini Hospital near Louis Trichardt after being mauled by a lion Tuesday. The park's senior conservation services manager, Bruce Bryden, said the incident happened at a ranger station halfway between Shingwedzi and Punda Maria camps. "Two rangers went jogging and noticed the lion lying in the road. They were attacked and Jinus Mangayne was bitten on the head, back and leg," Mr. Bryden said.

Sport Hunting and Poaching

Lions kill men and men kill lions. And there are many reasons why. In addition to the previously mentioned predators, humans also are in direct competition for food with lions. This competition leads to confrontations where man kills lions to protect livestock. He kills lions to protect himself. He kills lions to protect his family. He kills lions when accidentally confronted. And he kills lions for sport.

The great twentieth-century conservationist Aldo Leopold said:

Hunting is not merely an acquired taste; the instinct that finds delight in the sight and pursuit of game is bred into the very fiber of this race (man). We are dealing, therefore, with something that lies very deep. Some can live without opportunity for this exercise and control of the hunting instinct, just as I suppose some can live without work, play, love, business, or other vital adventures. But in these days we regard such deprivations as unsocial. Opportunity for exercise of all the normal instincts has come to be regarded more and more as an inalienable right.

The Citizen
August 18, 1993
GERMAN TOURIST KILLED BY LIONS
WINDHOEK — A young German tourist was killed by lions yesterday as he lay in his sleeping bag near a watering hole at the Etosha National Park. Mr. Martin Lenk, 24, of Niedernhall in Germany, was found dead in his sleeping bag. His neck had been broken, police said. "The lion and lioness entered the enclosure and killed Mr. Lenk by breaking his neck. The lions then proceeded to eat him," said Namibian Police spokesman, Chief Inspector Sean Geyser, in a statement. Police said Mr. Lenk, who was travelling with another German national, Mr. Andreas Abrell, was sleeping in the Okaukuejo Rest Camp, which is surrounded by a high wall to keep animals out. However, he was sleeping next to a watering hole, where the fence and a stone wall are much lower to enable tourists to watch animals drink. Another tourist sleeping on a bench nearby, was woken by a cry at 4 am, police said. The man saw a lioness sitting next to Mr. Lenk, who was in his sleeping bag. She was joined by an adult male lion. — Sapa-AP.

African professional hunters have, for the most part, a very ethical tradition. They adhere the regulations laid down by their respective governments. And they, as individuals and companies, in their own interest help to preserve the lions' unique environment.

One of the better photographic safaris I've been on was in an area of Tanzania that was owned by a hunting company. That company rewards local people for turning in snares, and sets aside income and donations from its hunting areas for anti-poaching projects. Poachers kill many times more animals in Africa than tourist hunters do, and the countries get no financial return from this poaching as they do from sport hunting. As an example, hunting the black rhinoceros has been outlawed for decades in all African countries. Not one rhino has been killed by sport hunters, but thousands have been slaughtered to the point of extinction by poachers just for the horns, which are sold to Asians as aphrodisiacs. Even when they want animals for food, their many indiscriminate snares kill thousands of game that are never retrieved. An American hunter may spend $50,000 just to hunt one elephant, while hundreds of others are killed by poachers with their government getting nothing. Eliminating poachers would greatly increase the number of animals in those areas.

Professional hunting does that. Then if the hunting companies turn part of a hunting area into a photographic zone, it has the same effect as increasing the size of a national park. Poaching was under reasonable control in Kenya until the government banned big game hunting in the 1970s. In Kenya, most of the elephants killed by poachers in the last hundred years died in the few years following that ban. Poaching is far less prevalent where hunting is allowed because hunters, being armed, can intimidate poachers who are killing their game animals.

In *At the Hand of Man*, an analysis of wildlife/human interactions that was lavishly praised in *The New York Times*, author Raymond Bonner notes that the chairman of the cat-specialist group of the International Union for the Conservation of Nature and Natural Resources (IUCN), Peter Jackson, admits that trophy hunting may be the only way to save some cat species.

Hunting provides many local incentives for assisting in conservation projects. But like any other group, hunters have their share of bad apples. There are strict quotas on the number of animals that can be taken within each concession. But if a rich hunter, for instance, bags a specimen on his first day out hunting, he may be tempted to find a larger animal later. If he succeeds in improving on his first kill, then the lesser trophy might be discreetly dumped. These unethical characters are rare, but their actions are volatile fodder for the anti-hunting fraternity.

Hunting for sport has been an urge in man for some time. It probably didn't take long for early subsistence hunters to enjoy the thrill facing off with a fierce animal "without effect" as Churchill said. The praise and gratitude the hunter received from his tribe-mates encouraged him in future engagements. It was just a matter of evolvement for it to be set in our psyche. Today's hunter still enjoys that primitive, personal satisfaction, although hunting with today's high-powered rifles and long-range telescopic sights is a far cry from a stone-age spear or bronze-age sword. These were real contact struggles with life-threatening hand-to-hand engagements every time. Today's hunter is probably less vulnerable when big game hunting than he or she is driving to work, but there is still the slight feeling of being close to primitive danger, which is gratifying to a hunter.

HUNTING THE LION

There are many methods of hunting lions, from the primitive, antagonizing and spearing practiced by some of the courageous tribes to today's posh safaris with high-powered rifles. One technique is spooring. Hunters find tracks early in the morning and follow them to the lion that is supposed to be sleeping in mid-day. There are, however, graves to prove that at least some lions did not read this script. Another is to follow a lion's roaring or grunting until he is encountered, usually by sight. A third method, baiting, entails leaving a dead animal tied to a tree in hopes that a lion shows up for a free meal. The lion is shot from a nearby blind or *machan*. Riding after lions on horseback is another effective, and exciting, method of hunting. I have been on horseback in the

African bush and it is a wonderful experience. On horseback you can approach game more closely. Hunters on horseback ride after lions—the fact that lions like to eat horses certainly gets one's blood moving—springing off when the lion stops and getting in the shot before the almost inevitable charge occurs. This method requires open country, such as the plains of East Africa, where, before the days of motor cars, it was fairly popular. Pilot and hunter Denys Finch Hatton, who helped open up the uncharted lands of East Africa for tourism and hunting, considered lion hunting on horse-back in Africa a first-class sport. "A gallop over rough country keeping one's eye on two or three lions at the same time and know-ing that a mistake meant fairly certain death, was a good deal more exciting than a ride around the park."

And from Colonel Stevenson-Hamilton: "It was thus in 1911 Mr. George Grey met his death. The secret of success in this form of sport apparently lies in never 'riding on the Lion's tail,' but in keeping wide on one flank, so that the pony may be swung round without losing his stride, in case of an unexpected rush by the lion." Grey did not. While on horseback a wealthy East African, Fritz Schindelar, had kept his eye on a fleeing lion and had not noticed another. It leaped at him and dragged him from his horse. He died in the hospital. The lion had torn out a large part of his intestines.

Although not done by "sportsmen," many lions were hunted with the help of dogs. This was a very effective way for villages to cure cheeky lions that had developed bad eating habits in their villagers.

American photographer, hunter, collector and adventurer Paul J. Rainey thought it would be nifty to hunt lion on horseback with dogs. He was struck down by a lion from his polo pony. "What a blow, what a blow," he kept saying as he was stretcher-borne from the scene. He died three days later from his wounds.

When in the Okavango in September 1999, I heard an account of a Botswana soldier eaten by lions when he was thrown from his horse and the rest of the armed soldiers fled and left him to his fate. I asked John Dugmore to trace the incident for me and it proved quite different from the rumor. The actual incident was in a fortnightly Botswana paper called *The Voice* dated 10th–23rd October, 1997. In an area near the Moremi Game Park, lions attacked a Botswana Defence Force (BDF) anti-poaching unit who were armed but on horseback. Two of the riders were thrown from the horses. Private Gaothobogwe was able to get up and run for his life, as the lions were distracted by the cries of twenty-three-year-old private Moses Mohinda. He was injured enough to pre-vent him from reaching his rifle and was immediately attacked and devoured by the lions. Private Norman, who kept control of his horse, was pursued by another lion, which was kicked in the face by the horse and returned to the rest of the lions and poor private Mohinda. The two surviving soldiers could not recover either their rifles or their dying comrade. Kalahari Conservation Society officer Dr. Keith Leggett said that it was the fourth lion attack on BDF patrols in 1998. He said that once lions eat human flesh they develop a taste for it, and in all likelihood they will kill humans again. "You don't want to take the chance of them becoming man-eaters." He said they posed a threat to the economy especially since the attack took place in an area visited by a lot of tourists. "You lose a couple of tourists to lions and you can kiss your tourist industry goodbye." No kidding.

Brian Marsh told me that lion hunters were employed on the newly settled cattle ranches of Southern Rhodesia (now Zimbabwe) in the early part of this century to dispatch cattle-killing lions. These ranches were situated in the low veld gamelands, and when first settled all carried a complement of wild game. To make room for cattle the grazers had to be disposed of. Zebra and wildebeest were shot where they were found. This was shortly to create its own problem. The lions, of which there was also a full complement, turned to killing cattle when their natural food began to dwindle.

John Alexander Hunter was born in Scotland before the turn of the last century. He recalled that soon after his arrival in Kenya as a very young man he hunted lions and shot elephants where towns now stand. When he was a guard on the first cross-country railroad between Nairobi and Mombasa, he depended upon the train driver giving "one hoot for a passenger to be picked up, two hoots when lions were sighted, and three hoots for a leopard."

The Pretoria News
October 9, 1984
LIONS ON THE RAMPAGE
LAGOS — Angry lions have terrorized villagers in Northern Nigeria, eating 23 cows and 10 goats, *The Daily Times* reported. The beasts had not yet turned man-eater, but inhabitants of Ari and Kafin Chiawa in Bauchi State were either hiding indoors or had taken refuge elsewhere, it said.

FIGHTING OFF LION ATTACKS

Pulp magazines used to fill their pages every month with hero hunters who killed dangerous game with a knife. Anyone who has seen a bear or big cat in a rage knows that this is rubbish. There are, of course, rare exceptions but they are with people whose work keeps them in close contact with such animals. If you hunt lions for a living, are a circus lion trainer or big cat zookeeper and see these big fellows at close quarters every day, then the law of averages is working against you. I very much doubt the believability of the stories about many casual hunters, who may hunt dangerous game just once in a while, having so many successful encounters with these big boys. Here are a few of those exceptions. Some were successful, some not.

In the early 1900s, Harry Wolhuter, the famous game ranger in South Africa's Kruger National Park, was attacked by a lion. He was pulled from his horse and dragged by his right shoulder, in excruciating pain. When he realized he might be eaten alive, he decided to stick his knife into the animal's heart. "The task was a difficult and complicated one because, gripped as I was, high up on the right shoulder, my head was pressed right up against the lion's mane, which exuded a strong lion smell and this necessitated my reaching with my left hand holding the knife across his chest so as to gain access to his left shoulder. Any bungling, in this maneuver, would arouse the lion, with instantly fatal results to myself!" Unbelievably, he succeeded in killing the lion.

It has often been said that a lion's victims feel nothing. David Livingstone, who was attacked by a lion in Bechuanaland (now Botswana), wrote this account:

> *growling horribly close to my ear, he shook me as a terrier does a rat. The shock produced a stupor... a sort of dreaminess in which there was no sense of pain or feeling of terror, though quite conscious of all that was happening. It was like what patients partially under the influence of chloroform describe, who see all the operation, but feel not the knife... This singular condition was not the result of any mental process. The shake annihilated fear and allowed no sense of horror in looking around at the beast."*

The Hungarian naturalist, Kittenburger, who was badly mauled in Tanzania, also felt "no pain at all." Others have told of similar experiences. On the other hand, C. Cronje Wilmot, a Ngamiland tsetse fly control officer who was mauled and wounded twenty-three times in one attack, records feeling intense pain. Arnold Wienholt, of Australia, and Petros Jacobs, who were attacked at different times, recall terrible pain— "like having nine-inch nails driven into you," said Wienholt. Game warden Bruneau de Laborie of French Equatorial Africa died weeks after receiving a bite on the arm from a lion and reported great pain. In recent years, the use of antibiotics has undoubtedly saved hundreds from death by infection.

Theodore Roosevelt describes, in his *African Game Trails,"* an incident with Carl Akeley, the genius who was responsible for the wonderful African Hall at the American Museum of Natural History. "My friend, Carl Akeley, of Chicago, actually killed bare-handed a leopard which sprang on him. Akeley actually choked and crushed the life out of it, although his arm was badly bitten. A leopard will charge at least as readily as one of the big beasts, and is rather more apt to get his charge home, but the risk is less to life than to limb."

In June 1993, a lioness crept up and grabbed the sleeping bag of South African Defence Force Riflemen Shaun Pautz and David Roussouw while they were sleeping. Roussouw woke up screaming, and Pautz screamed and waved his arms to chase the lioness away. The lioness grabbed Pautz by the boot before running off with the boot. While the soldiers were carrying rifles, they were not allowed to shoot animals. How's that for obeying orders?

Inside a private game reserve in northern Natal, an elderly Durban woman had left the cocktail area to go and freshen up before dinner. A few minutes later, her husband went looking for her. Rangers in the boma heard a thud and a cry, and immediately rushed out to see what had happened. In the torchlight, on the path between the boma and swimming pool, they saw a lioness standing over the body of the husband, Mr. Strous. The lioness ran when she saw the rangers who rushed to the badly mauled man. The rangers then went a little further up the path to see if there

Agitated Elephants, Oil on Canvas

Daily News Reporter
September 13, 1982

THREE MEN BITTEN IN NATAL LION ATTACKS

Three men were mauled by lionesses in separate attacks on the same day at the Natal game reserves recently. One of the victims, Mr. Isiah Hkosi (36), a former labourer on the canefields, is still recovering from wounds on his left leg and arm after being bitten by an adult lioness, near his home bordering the Hluhluwe Game Reserve. Moments earlier his friend, Mr. Alpheus Thabethe (30) was attacked by the same lioness and on the same day Mr. Wyoand Kanfer, a trail officer with the Natal Parks Board, was also mauled by an adult lioness at the Umfolosi Game Reserve. "I came across him lying on the ground. He appeared shocked and was in pain. I asked him what had happened and he said he had been attacked by a 'big animal'," Mr. Nkosi said. "Not realizing it could be a lion I went to see if the animal was still about. Then it came at me from the bushes and pinned me to the ground." Mr. Nkosi said the lioness bit his thigh and then tried to bite his neck, but he warded it off with his arm, which was also bitten. "I went limp, as if I were dead, and after several minutes the lioness, which sat on me all this time, wandered off."

were any other lions in the area and found the partially eaten body of Mrs. Strous.

In Jan Hemsing's book, *Encounters with Lions,* Anthony Seth-Smith was hunting with two American clients and another professional hunter named Rene Babault. At night they liked to sleep with the flaps of their tents rolled up, the better to savor the night. They heard lions roaring and intended to sit awake and watch to see if they came through the camp. A lion sniffed at one tent and then came across to the mouth of Babault's tent. After staring at him for a long time, the lion made a dash for the end of his bed, grabbed Babault's shorts, ran off with them, and never came back. Again in the same book was this encounter: Allan Earnshaw of Ker & Downey (Kenya) tells of an incident when a lion walked right through the gathering of safari clients and game warden as they were sitting around the campfire. The lion walked up to the cook, grabbed him, and proceeded to devour him in front everyone.

The clients got quite hysterical and the game ranger was encouraged at this point to fire upon the beast which he couldn't do immediately. It was too difficult to decide where the beast was and where the cook was (whom the lion was eating), but eventually he fired two or three shots, but missed completely because he was shaking too much. One of the clients then, who had done quite a lot of deer hunting, wrested the rifle from the ranger's hand and took aim and fired, but nothing happened. The fellow had only had three bullets. They had to continue to watch the gruesome spectacle to the end, they were quite helpless.

There is a story of a herdsman on a cattle ranch in the Kedong Valley who was attacked by a lion. The lion bit him and was standing over the poor chap who had fallen to the ground. The lion's head was growling over the herdsman's feet. He was afraid to call to his friends for fear of angering the lion more. The lion's tail was whipping back and forth almost in front of his nose. Desperate, he bit the tail as hard as he could. The lion ran off in complete surprise.

All the big cats are dormant disasters waiting for some unexplained trigger to set them off. Siegfried and Roy had the most successful show in Las Vegas history. It was a most amazing animal illusion act and they were known for how well they treated their big cats. Roy was mauled by one of his most trusted pets which had been on stage with him for five years. During a performance in the fall of 2003, the tiger unexpectedly growled. The cat was somehow distracted by a woman in the front row. Roy pulled on the tiger's chain and swiftly moved to block its view of the woman. At that point the 600 pound cat grabbed Horn's arm. Roy bopped him on the nose. Then, witnesses agree, Roy stumbled, and the cat pounced, biting into Roy's neck. Seconds later, reverting to routine, it exited stage left, dragging Roy by the throat. Backstage, the crew sprayed the cat with a fire extinguisher. Releasing his victim the tiger retired to his cage.

Roy raised the cat at his opulent home in Las Vegas. Siegfried and Roy "are known for the care they give to their animals," said John Seidensticker, a tiger specialist with the Smithsonian National Zoological Park, "tigers are specialized predators of large mammals. No matter how well you know your animal, there are circumstances that can set this off." That night it was — the woman? the microphone?" The tiger was definitely annoyed, says Mel Sunquist, a carnivore specialist at the University of Florida, "but if this animal had intended to kill Roy, Roy would now be dead. There is no doubt." Montecore came close: Backstage after the attack, with a gaping puncture wound to his neck, Roy's life was seeping out on the floor: By the time Roy arrived at University Medical Center's trauma unit seven minutes later, "he was still talking, still breathing," By press time Roy had suffered two strokes.

Donald Ker was sleeping under an open tent on one occasion and woke up to see the face of a lioness sitting at his feet. She was right under the tent fly. He spoke to her quietly so he wouldn't startle her and shone a flashlight into her eyes. The lioness walked away and joined her family lying a few yards from the tent. He then banged a metal container and the whole pride moved on. Despite many lion encounters, Ker's partner Syd Downey considered African bees as dangerous as any of the "Big Five," (buffalo, lion, elephant, leopard, and rhino). Botswana's Pat Hepburn told me that safari ants could be even worse. Personally, I am quite prepared to take their word for it.

Most fatal accidents with lions happen when the human has been guilty of misjudgment. Lions have probably held man in respect since the early cave dwellers, whose crude weapons and great cunning made man a formidable adversary. The big cats learned to avoid us since we weren't worth the trouble that usually came. Misjudgment, however, depends on the individual. Lions' respect for man must have greatly increased over the last few hundred years, when the firearm became commonplace on the African continent.

Man-Eating Lions

The lion is second only to the crocodile as a man-eater in Africa. Hippos may kill more humans but don't eat them. Few lions, though, have man-eating inclinations. The tiny exception however, causes us to look at lions with slightly wider eyes. I personally feel that most any lion can become a man-eater under the right circumstances, especially if it is hungry enough. The custom so many tribes have of leaving their dead, and even their dying, outside the villages to be eaten by carrion eaters provides tempting opportunities for lions, which can easily acquire a taste for people. When the rains come, grass grows too high for the lion to easily hunt its normal prey. During this period, some appear to turn man-eater. The disappearance of game through hunting, snaring, and veld fires may also force lions to hunt either livestock or humans. Man-eating frequently flares up after human catastrophes such as wars or epidemics when, presumably, dead or dying people are in abundant supply.

What makes one area attractive to man-eaters and others not? I suspect that in Central Africa one cause was the Arab slave trade. Over the course of three centuries, Arab slave traders left hundreds of thousands of unwanted captives to die near their villages and thousands more beside the well-beaten slave trails that cut through the hostile African bush. Lions, leopards, and hyenas cleaned practically all of them up. Since the Arabs were taking the cream of the African tribes, those few weaker tribesmen not fit for the Arabs were left behind, and were powerless to keep back the wild animals. Man-eating became habitual among the big cats and there is still evidence of this today. Writer and professional hunter John Taylor observed that on the Revugwi River, near its confluence with the Zambezi, one could shoot out all the man-eaters, but sooner or later they would reappear. Old age and injuries force lions to pursue weaker prey, which may restart the man-eating cycle.

At the turn of the previous-or-twentieth century large numbers of natives were killed by lions along the Beira Railway line. The lions patrolled it regularly and a number of them were shot. Parties went out from Beira and other towns especially to hunt them.

J.A. Hunter describes one occasion with Major David Sheldrick, a warden of Tsavo National Park. "I sat up all night by a fine zebra, hoping to get a lion or two. No luck attended us, although during the night we heard lions grunting and the giggling sounds hyena make when on something they like particularly. Our bait was not touched. I had thought it represented what lions and hyena were most attracted by. I had something to learn." The Masai natives laid their failure to an elderly Masai lady who had been put out in the bush to die and had been eaten during the previous evening. It was she upon whom the *liwaru* and *majeannies* (lion and hyena) had been feeding."To me the hard way of life among primitive people seems stickily grim. Beasts of the wild preferred an old Masai woman to a fat juicy zebra," continued Sheldrick. The business of leaving the old and sick out to die by many tribes struggling for survival is common. It is their way of handling those who cannot contribute to the tribe any longer. It is also of course another contributing factor in putting man on the lion's menu.

A.J Siggins said man-eating by lions was very common before Europeans came to Africa. It was particularly bad in Mozambique when he was there. Man-eaters were very troublesome all along the coast between Palma and the M'Salu. Women were taken when fetching water or firewood men were taken, particularly when alone in the bush, whether hunting or visiting nearby villages. Natives never traveled at night when a lion scare was on. Doors were barred and men took weapons when traveling or working in isolated areas in daylight. In order to avoid the cover where lions could wait in ambush they would walk along beaches instead of bush paths, even if it took them many hours longer. Siggins was asked to kill two man-eating lions that were terrorizing the footpath between Miromvi and Palma. Natives haad to make a detour of two days' journey through the hills at the back, or else make the journey by sea. The lions had killed a woman who straggled behind her group where the path ran through a swamp. The lions, which had followed the party, jumped her and carried her off.

The Pretoria News
October 23, 1990

LIONESS MAULS GAME RANGER AT KRUGER PARK CAMP

JOHANNESBURG — A lioness has attacked and mauled a game ranger at the Mopani Camp in the Kruger National Park. The ranger, Mr. Kobus Botha, managed to save his face from serious injury by pushing his right hand down the lioness's throat, before she was shot dead by another game ranger. Mr. Botha's left leg and right hand were severely injured in the attack. A helicopter was sent from Skukuza and took him to the Palaborwa Hospital. His condition was described last night as satisfactory. Senior ranger Dirk Stewart said Mr. Botha encountered the lioness in the camp at first light, and tried to coax her out of the camp. At one point the lioness had been cornered. She charged Mr. Botha and knocked him down as he fired a shot. Mr. Stewart said the shot severed the lioness's shoulder tendon and she was only able to use one paw. Last Sunday a hiking party was charged by two lionesses near Satara in the south of the reserve. A ranger shot one lioness. No one was injured. The Mopani Camp is a new tourist camp currently under construction.

Siggins also believed that once lions start eating man, they very quickly develop a taste for human flesh.

In his book, *Out in the Midday Shade*, Bill York describes one un-provoked lion attack. I was asking him for some non-hunting lion stories and he sent me his wonderful book. Here is one incident that happened in camp at night:

Making as little sound as possible, I reached for my .404; unlike my double, this gun was always kept loaded. As I grasped it I received a hard blow to my elbow, which knocked the rifle from my hand. At the same time I heard a loud grunt, followed by a frightful scream from Musa [Bill's cook]. There was some thrashing about and continued screaming mingled with the furious grunts of a lion, which moved away from camp for a few yards. I yelled to the others to climb the trees and shot up one myself, feeling quite helpless as my .404 had disappeared in the dark. The screams abruptly ceased and were followed by horrid crunching and lapping sounds; the lion was eating Musa no more than twenty-five yards from where we were cowering in the thorny branches. The crunching sounds continued for what seemed several hours, although it could not have been for more than about thir-

ty minutes, after which the lion dragged away Musa's remains. We were left on our inglorious perches to while away the interminable hours of darkness. Despite the acute discomfort of our positions, I instructed the others to remain where they were. Although I had heard only one lion, it was possible that others were prowling around. It would have been the height of folly to risk losing another man, or myself, by descending before daylight.

Engineer, interpreter, explorer, and big game hunter of the last century, Arthur H. Neumann, said that cattle- and man-eating lions in his area were created by drought and burned-out grass areas. It became extremely difficult for their normal prey to feed, thereby making it hard for the lions to acquire game.

The indomitable big game hunter F.C. Selous had most of his man-eating lion experiences with those that were hurt:

The teeth of this lioness were worn down to mere stumps, and there is no doubt that the infirmities of old age, and the lack of strength requisite to catch and kill wild animals, had driven her to attack a human being. A hungry lion is a true devil, and fears nothing in this world. The fact that one does not hear of regular man-eating lions, that for a long period have been in the habit of preying upon human beings, as is the case with tigers in India, is due, I fancy, not to the difference in the nature of the animals, but to the superior boldness of the African natives over those of India. Amongst such warlike tribes as Matabele, if a lion only kills an ox, or even a goat, its fate is usually sealed.

Sunday Star
October 7, 1984
LIONS, HIPPO MAUL "EDEN" VISITORS
FRANCISTOWN — Botswana is living up to its claim of being an "untamed Eden." Lions and a hippo have killed a 17-year-old girl and critically injured two men in the past five weeks. Both John Chase, who was mauled by a lion on Tuesday, and the Motswana farmer who was trampled by a hippo had to be flown to South Africa for treatment. On August 29 a lion wandered into the camp of a party of German tourists in the Moremi Game Reserve and dragged teenager Karina Broums out of her tent. The lion towed Karina across a stream and, watched by Karina's horrified campmates, tore chunks of flesh from her legs on the far bank. Warden Andrew Chwene eventually shot the lion. Last year he and his colleagues were woken by the screams of a poacher who had been grabbed by a lion. They ran up shouting and the lion backed off.

Such a thing as a man-eater, or even an habitual cattle-slayer, would never be tolerated for an instant.

But it is significant that a great many hunters describe man-eaters as being in good condition. The Njombe man-eaters and the Tsavo man-eaters were very healthy specimens. It certainly goes against the theory that man-eaters are forced to eat people because they are either too old or too crippled to hunt. A lot of sick lions do turn man-eater, of course, but sickness is not as important a cause of man-eating as many people believe. But as in the case of the Njombe man-eaters, some have never hunted anything else but humans. They were born to man-eating parents, who weaned them on human flesh and taught them the art of stalking men. These can be the most difficult to eliminate.

When Fred Bartlett was a child with his parents, they were sleeping near the Mozambique border with Rhodesia (now Zimbabwe). A man-eating lion had jumped on the roof of a local native hut, clawed through the thatch, grabbed a woman and jumped out with her. It made a big impression on him. Later in his career, Fred was to go after many man-eaters. Jim Corbett was

sort of his role model. Fred, a very healthy big fellow, told me that Corbett was a small person and looked very unimposing, and he found it hard to believe that he very successfully hunted man-eating tigers and leopards. In his book *Shoot Straight and Stay Alive*, Fred describes the lengths they went to in eliminating man-eaters. A warden, Tom Salmon, was called out to deal with a lioness, which had killed and eaten the younger wife of a chief. This occurred just below Meru. It was late in the day and in a very short time darkness would fall. Tom realized that the lioness would return shortly and the only action he could take was to put strychnine in the body. He turned to the chief and asked permission to use his dead wife's body. He agreed and said, "By all means, she is no good to me anymore!" Tom put poison in the body and the next day the lioness was found dead close by.

Frank C. Hibben wrote of a large male lion that had killed a woman and her twelve-year-old daughter just north of Tabda in Somalia. Apparently the lion had killed the girl first, as she herded a little flock of sheep toward the water. The Somali woman had rushed to drive the lion away from her daughter, and the lion had killed her also. "The lion had dragged the girl beneath the brush at the side of the trail and had almost completely devoured her. Other herdsmen had found her chewed and bloody clothes there. The woman had been killed by a blow of the lion's paw and a bite through the base of the neck; but had not been eaten. The fat-tailed sheep still grazed around the spot where the bodies lay," Hibben wrote. The sheep were completely ignored by the lion.

While at the Tony Dyer home in the highlands of Kenya, Tony explained how there may well be room for the lion in modern Africa, but how there will not be enough land for the animals he must eat. If it does not have enough wild prey to eat, the lion turns to cattle and to man, and is then destroyed. In Dyer's area of Kenya, invariably the man-eating lion either is hungry because there is no wild game in its range, or because he has been injured so that he cannot kill wild game. Southern Tanzania has had man-eating lions for many years. After poachers and locals killed much of the game, the lions were left without their normal prey and turned to domestic stock and then humans. As Schaller pointed out, the lions found out how easy it was to pick off drunken locals or those who visited neighboring villages at night. I had been near

(Newspaper and date unknown)

KILLER LION

Actor-director Clint Eastwood this week moved his movie team on to Zimbabwe's Fothergill Island on Lake Kariba, undeterred by a hunt nearby for a man-eating lion. The man-eater, nicknamed Maswerasei by local villagers, had terrorized the south shore in the Ume communal area, killing and eating one schoolgirl and mauling several others. The lion's name means "Have you had a nice day?" in Shona, the standard afternoon greeting, referring to the beast's habit of blatant daylight attacks. Although Clint's team will be sleeping under canvas on Fothergill for the filming of *White Hunter, Black Heart*, a story based on the making of *The African Queen*, safari men believe Eastwood and his crew are quite safe from the lion.

Secretary Bird, Oil on Canvas

The Citizen
May 2, 1998
US HIKER FIGHTS OFF LION WITH BARE HANDS

DENVER - A 24-year-old man hiking through a state park in Colorado fought off a mountain lion by poking his thumb in the cat's eye and stabbing it with a small knife, the *Denver Post* reported yesterday. The attack occurred on Thursday afternoon after a 30-minute standoff along a hiking trail on Carpenter Peak in Roxborough Park in Douglas County, south of Denver, officials said. It was the first recorded attack on a human by a mountain lion in the park's 11-year history, the paper said. The hiker, whose name was not released, suffered deep cuts to his head and face, but was able to run down the trail and call for help after fighting off the cat. He was hospitalized in stable condition. "He did everything right, that's why he survived," a spokesman said. "He didn't run, he fought back."

one native bar near Lake Manyara at the time he describes that a native who had had too much to drink was caught by a lion on his way home. Now there's a very convincing reason to stop drinking.

Rinderpest is a highly infectious and deadly disease of grazing animals. It swept the continent in the 1890s, it traveled up the Nile, devastated East and Central Africa, and reached South Africa within seven years. No one knows how many animals died in the Serengeti, but the numbers must have been staggering. Wildebeest, giraffe, warthog, buffalo, and gazelle were all hit hard. Ungrazed grasslands turned into bush, and tsetse flies and sleeping sickness soon followed. People were crushed by famine. Lions sought alternative prey, and many became man-eaters. Denys Finch Hatton thought that lions were more aggressive in the partially settled districts because game was scarce in those settlements. They then find it very easy to prey on local cattle. In proximity to villages and cattle, sooner or later a lion kills a herdsman or a village boy and becomes a qualified man-eater. But in the real wilderness Hatton felt it was very rare for a lion, other than a wounded one, to attack humans.

A healthy lion that has become a man-eater would need a minimum of fifty victims a year to stay alive, and a hundred and fifty to remain in peak condition. C.J.P. Ionides, one of Africa's man-eater hunters, describes a lion that ate a fat woman and then a warthog "for dessert." That probably was not at the same sitting. Individual lions have killed and eaten as many as three people in a single night.

For a person who has never seen a wild lion, it is difficult to appreciate how enormously powerful they are. For a creature that is capable of killing a buffalo weighing almost a ton, a man is a small fry. Lions have been known to carry victims for up to a mile without a rest. One judiciously placed bite, usually in the neck or head, can kill instantly. A single blow that can break an ox's neck will easily break a man's back. It is difficult to rank the lion by the number of kills among the man-eaters of the world. Since lions usually hunt in prides, it is just about impossible to establish what any individual lion ate. The solitary leopards and tigers are easier to identify with a body count for one specific killer in its particular area. More on them later.

Man-eating lions display odd characteristics that are not found in normal lions. One of the most pronounced is their habit of usually moving as far away from the kill as possible before dawn. They might cover twenty miles after eating a victim. A man-eater can range over hundreds of square miles. It is hard to tell whether it does this knowing that this movement makes it almost impossible to track, or, having struck a village once, it knows there is little chance of catching another victim so easily. Another idiosyncrasy is the man-eater's reluctance to eat anything but human flesh once that taste is acquired, and he or she has enormous patience in seeking it.

Perhaps the oddest characteristic of all is the extraordinary lengths to which lions go to get a particular victim. Patterson describes how one of the Tsavo lions would step right over a sleeping man in order to get at another beyond him. Ionides suggests it might be due to a difference in each man's smell and lions have remarkable noses. They may very well prefer the safer, less aggressive prey that eat fish than the more aggressive prey that eat meat, and are able to tell the difference by their scent. I will go into more detail on this later, on page 137. I strongly suggest, however, that lions have some form of this capability.

Quite often, once a lion has set its sights upon a specific victim, it will attempt to tear doors down to get at him, and burning torches will not deter him. In Kenya, according to Ionides, a man-eater entered a ring of blazing fire to snatch up a sleeping man. Taylor describes how a man on a bicycle rode down a hill straight between two man-eaters. The lions pulled the next cyclist down and ate him. Schaller describes instances of man-eating lions in the 1960s, at Lake Manyara Park in Tanzania, where he was doing some research. There was plenty of game of all kinds readily available. Several villagers had been injured, and in July, 1969, a man was caught at night and almost wholly eaten. Schaller was staying at Lake Manyara Lodge at the time, and he was warned not to be out when it was dark. Two more killings occurred in the ensuing months, and in May, 1970, Makacha, Schaller's assistant, wrote to him: "Satima, the young male among the Mahali pa Nyati pride, has been shot when he was found eating another killed person near the Park Headquarters." These lions had ample food in the form of buffalo and impala available.

In January 1997, on New Year's Day, a lion ate a family of four in a village west of the Tanzanian capital, Dar Es Salaam. The lion pounced on and killed the man, his wife, and their two children. The incident occurred in Kidegede village in Tanzania's Kilombero district. In October 1996, tourists were having their evening meal at the Santawani camp in Botswana's Moremi game reserve. As they walked from the dining area to the campfire to have coffee, the tourists heard the screams of assistant chef Frans Galeshiwe. The camp manager, Bruce Muller, grabbed a rifle and torch and killed the lioness. The next day, game rangers shot another lioness that apparently had been injured in a fight. A large number of lions, all thin from lack of food because of the drought, were in the area at the time.

Alan Black's long career as a hunter in Kenya started in 1903 after service in the Boer War, when he was hired by Lord Delamere to shoot for the pot to keep his porters fed. He wore a hat decorated with the tail tips of fourteen man-eaters he had killed. In May 1981, something was killing chickens and ducks penned near a family's hut in the Dande tribal reserve in northeastern Zimbabwe. Three children, alone and thinking the animal was a hyena, shouted to scare it off. It wasn't a hyena. A lion rushed the hut, killed the children, and ate them. When their mother returned later that night, the lion, still feeding in the hut, killed and ate her as well, and then left.

Amateur ornithologist, British Col. Richard Meinertzhagen, who spent so much time in Africa, said the man-eaters of Thika had accounted for more than fifty Africans. On one of their attempts to get the lions, they encountered a pair of them. "If he did make up his mind to fire he should have shot the lioness, as they are always the most dangerous: it is well known that a lioness will often charge, if her spouse is fired at." I'm glad I was unaware of that in 1993 when, on a hunting safari with a client, I found myself running through a pride of lionesses trying to keep up with the hunters chasing the male. Fortunately for me, I suppose, the male had not been fired upon. Those lionesses were but thirty paces from us on either side and to this day I wonder why they didn't either run away or attack us. They just watched as if we were birds flying by.

In his book *African Game Trails,* Theodore Roosevelt said that "During the last three or four years, in German and British East Africa and Uganda, over fifty white men have been killed or mauled by lions." With so few whites in that part of Africa at the time, can you imagine what the total was for the natives? It is the middle of Africa, however, that probably suffers more than any other area from the depredations of man-eating lions. The most notorious part includes the Southern Province of Tanzania (formerly Tanganyika), the north of Malawi (formerly Nyasaland), and the northern section of Mozambique. This region has bred such delinquents as the terrible man-eaters of Njombe. A trademark of these particular man-eaters was their love of human brains, with every victim's skull carefully bitten open and licked clean of its contents. As is also often the case with confirmed man-eaters, they would eat nothing but humans, disdaining cattle, goats, and even chickens in their fondness for human meat. Editor James Clark reported that in the Mafienge district (just outside the Southern Province) two lions killed twenty-three people in about two months. It is slightly northeast of the corner where Zambia, Malawi, and Tanzania come together in your atlas. This occurred " at the edge of the mountainous highlands in what's called the Buhoro Flats, and it was in this great sun-seared snarl of thorn-fanged nyika that most of the killings were conducted."

In the Lindi district just above Mozambique, according to Guggisberg, four pairs of man-eaters patrolled the Nyangao-Massissi road in search of victims. They have a special drum in these parts called *ngula mtwe* (it means "a man is eaten") and its somber beat comprises two short thumps followed by a long one. Just south of this region, over the Mozambique border, Austin Roberts and Vaughan Kirby hunted down four man-eaters that were eating twenty people a month. In some parts, villages were abandoned from time to time when man-eating got really bad, and even the local style of architecture shows certain modifications to protect against persistent man-eaters who might try to rip open a hut to get at the inhabitants. Two of the worst areas in Central Africa used to be the Luangwa Valley in Zambia (formerly Northern Rhodesia) and central Malawi (Nyasaland), where after the Second World War, a single lion ate fourteen people in a month. John Taylor once shot five man-eaters at Nsungu on the north

Lion Around II, Oil on Canvas

bank of the Zambesi. He shot three as they tried to tear the door off his hut. Over a period of time at Mikindani in the south, one lion is known to have accounted for 380 victims.

The Tsavo area of East Africa is known as an occasional haven for man-eating lions. Here, dozens of workers were eaten during the building of the railway from the coast at Mombasa through to Uganda. Some people believe that the bout of man-eating was triggered by the quantity of fever victims whose bodies had been thrown into the bush avoiding burial. But Tsavo was notorious long before the railway was built, and has been hunted by a few man-eaters since those unhappy times. In 1955, a telegram was received in Nairobi from a Tsavo railway official who wrote, "Odeke narrowly escaped being caught by lion... all staff unwilling to do night duty. Afford protection." Major Robert Foran shot four man-eaters in one day near this area after the lions had killed fifty people in three months. Since the Second World War, however, there has been only one case reported. An emaciated lion (380 pounds) was shot at Darajani, not far up the railway line from Tsavo, in 1965. John Kingsley-Heath, who shot it, told me he had found a porcupine quill rammed into its nostril.

The Ankole district of Uganda, just west of Lake Victoria, also has a bad reputation. The Sariga area of Ankole is particularly notorious and in the 1920s, according to Guggisberg, bands of man-eaters roamed over hundreds of square miles. One of them accounted for eighty-four victims while another ate forty-four. Their depredations spread to Entebbe, on the north shore of Lake Victoria. This particular reign of terror ended after seventeen lions had been shot. But in 1938 another began. Guggisberg attributed the outbreak to rinderpest, which had killed off the game, forcing the lions to eat cattle and have closer conflicts with man.

The tenacity and cunning of a man-eating lion is extraordinary. Take this incident, in June 1900, at Kima Station in the Congo, west of Africa's Great Lakes system, written about in James Clarke's *Man is the Prey*.

> *The lion attempted to tear through the corrugated iron roof of a station building and eventually succeeded in carrying off a railway driver, but the man managed to squeeze into a galvanized iron tank. For several minutes the lion tried to hook him out by placing its paw through a hole like a bear at a honey pot. Superintendent Ryall of the Railway Police decided to have a try at shooting the beast and had his personal railway carriage shunted onto the siding. Two others, Hubner and Parenti, joined him. The three men occupied one compartment, and Ryall took first watch by sitting on a bunk in the compartment and keeping watch out of the open window. The two others slept, Parenti on the floor and Hubner on a high bunk.*
>
> *Ryall must have nodded off to sleep. The lion, either by luck or incredible intelligence entered the carriage undetected at one end, padded softly down the corridor and slid the door open. Hubner woke up, and saw the lion below him straddling Parenti, who was lying motionless but awake. The lion reached across the compartment, swiped Ryall across the side of the head (probably killing him instantly) and sank its fangs into his chest near the left armpit. Hubner leaped over the lion's back and tried to escape through the sliding door leading into the corridor, but frantic tribesmen, knowing what was inside, were keeping it shut. Suddenly there was a crash, and Hubner looked over his shoulder to see the lion leap through the window with Ryall in its jaws. Parenti, his Latin excitement getting the better of him, also leaped out of the window. The lion had been standing on him. The man-eater was later caught in a trap and was put on show until it was shot a day or so later.*

Englishman Stephen Bagnal in 1902 was dragged from his tent and eaten by a lion. There was nothing of him left but his boots.

Guggisberg tells of an African near Fort Mangoche, Malawi,

The Pretoria News
May 11, 1989
RAINCOAT SAVES MAN
FROM LIONESS ATTACK
NELSPRUIT — Shortly after
entering the reserve he [Mr.
Mongwe] spotted two lions, a
lioness and a number of cubs
less than 3 meters away. As
the cubs playfully ran towards
him the lioness growled,
lurched forward and grabbed
Mr. Mongwe by the left arm.
"While she pulled at my arm I
quickly unbuttoned my coat,
slipped it off and managed to
get away," Mr. Mongwe said.
As the lioness and her cubs
ripped at the coat, Mr.
Mongwe, standing some distance away, shouted and threw
stones at them. Still growling,
she gathered her cubs and
slowly walked away with the
other lions. Bleeding and in
pain, Mr. Mongwe walked
through the night and reached
the Nwanetsi camp the following morning.

Major Stewart's Pith Helmet, Oil on Canvas

who was attacked outside his hut. This hut was isolated from the village. His wife rushed at the lion with a firebrand and the lion dropped the man. The woman dragged her husband inside and bolted the door. He died a few minutes later. Meanwhile the lion was attacking the door, trying to tear it down. The woman picked up a firebrand once more and rushed out into the night. The lion then re-entered the hut and carried off its victim.

This lion's tenacity is described by Theodore Roosevelt :

> *There was an askari on duty; yet a lion crept up, entered the tent, and seized and dragged forth the man. He struggled and made outcry; there was a rush of people, and the lion dropped his prey and bounded off. The man's wounds were dressed, and he was put back to bed in his own tent; but an hour or two after the camp again grew still, the lion returned, bent on the victim of whom he had been robbed; he re-entered the tent, seized the unfortunate wounded man with his great fangs, and this time made off with him into the surrounding darkness, killed and ate him. Not far from the scene of this tragedy, another had occurred. An English officer named Stewart, while endeavoring to kill his first lion, was himself set on and slain.*

Today man-eating lions are still very busy. In South Africa's Kruger Park alone, according to *The Johannesburg Star*, August 6, 1998, seven people were killed and eaten in 1997 and four more were killed to that date in 1998. Dr. Willem Gertenbach, the park's general manager of nature conservation, says most casualties are never reported because what the lions don't finish the hyenas and vultures do. Occasionally, human fingers are found in wild lion feces.

In *Simba*, Guggisberg points out that prompt action can sometimes save a man-eater's prey. Many victims remain alive for some time after being carried off. There was a case involving a man in German East Africa (Tanzania) who called in vain for fifteen min-utes while literally being eaten alive. Again in German East Africa, Hans Blesser mentions in James Clark's book how he stood by helplessly while a villager was dragged screaming into the bush by a man-eater. He got volunteers together and they advanced on the lion that, with determined charges, drove them back time after time. All the while, says Blesser, the victim moaned for help or screamed when the harried lion fed on him. The next day his body was found abandoned, intact except what the lion ate, only a thigh and a calf. As dangerous as they can be, consider the incident from the beginning of this book where the lioness and cubs encountered the European woman and her two children. What made the lioness so non-violent? You just don't know how any particular lion will react in any given situation.

TSAVO - NJOMBE LIONS

Prides rather than solitary lions do most of the large volume of man-eating on the African continent. The Njombe man-eaters numbered fifteen at the height of their pride. There were even more Ankole man-eaters. The Tsavo killers were two huge maneless lions, nothing at all like those in the recent movie, *The Ghost and the Darkness*. These two lions alone were responsible for the deaths of "28 Indian coolies and scores of unfortunate African natives of whom no official record was kept," according to J.H. Patterson. Along the total rail distance between Mombasa and Entebbe, he killed a total of eight lions that were thought to be man-eaters. The reason the Tsavo lions were all the rage was not just that they ate so many natives and coolies, but that they actually stopped the building of the line at the Tsavo Bridge, 132 miles from the coast. What does the word Tsavo mean? It is the Masai word for "*slaughter*."

Patterson's *The Man-Eaters of Tsavo* has become one of the classic collector's books on Africa. Patterson is recognized as one of the great adventurers in the opening of East Africa. An engineer engaged in the construction of the Uganda Railway, Patterson endured a job hazard seldom encountered in the construction business —a plague of lions that had developed a taste for his coolie labor. It was a problem that could hardly be solved by either arbitration or negotiation. Patterson, a modest man but a singularly brave one, approached the situation as he would any logistical or building problem: He solved it by removing the cause of the trouble. In the process, he was very nearly "removed" himself.

No book in the field of big game hunting gives as vivid a description of the terror created by man-eating lions as does Patterson's classic. His account of a typical raid also serves to show the absolute fearlessness of some man-eaters:

> *The two brutes made a most ferocious attack on the largest camp in the section, which for safety's sake was situated within a stone's throw of Tsavo Station and close to a Permanent Way Inspector's iron hut. Suddenly, in the dead of night, the two man-eaters burst in among the terrified workmen, and even from my* boma, *some distance away, I could plainly hear the panic-stricken shrieking of the coolies. Then followed cries of "They've taken him; they've taken him," as the brutes carried off their unfortunate victim and began their horrible feast close beside the camp.*

The Inspector and Patterson fired more than fifty shots in the direction from which they heard the lions, but the lions were not frightened and calmly lay there until their meal was finished. In the morning, Patterson and some of the others set off to track the lions.

> *Inspector Dalgairns believed he had wounded one and pointed to a dragging trail which could have been a lion's foot. After some careful stalking, we suddenly found ourselves in the vicinity of the lions, and were greeted with ominous growling. Cautiously advancing and pushing the bushes aside, we saw in the gloom what we at first took to be a lion cub; closer inspection showed it to be the remains of the unfortunate coolie, which the man-eaters had evidently abandoned at our approach. The legs, one arm and half the body had been eaten, and it was the stiff fingers on the other arm trailing along the sand which had left the marks we had taken to be the trail of a wounded lion.*

The lions got away and the coolies went on strike. Work on the Uganda Railway came to a standstill and the killings continued night after night. Not one lion had been killed. Soon after this, Patterson called in a Mr. Whitehead, who, on the night he arrived at Tsavo, was ambushed by a lion which succeeded in clawing his back in the darkness. Whitehead's gun went off in the fracas, and the lion switched back to its attack on Whitehead's *askari*, Abdullah. "*Eh, Bwana, simba!*" was all the *askari* had time to say. He was eaten. The following night Patterson sat up in a *machan*. It was dark and the silence flooded in.

> *A deep long drawn sigh—sure sign of hunger—came up from the bushes, and the rustling commenced again as [the lion] cautiously advanced. In a moment or two a sudden stop, followed by an angry growl, told me that my presence had been noticed, and I began to fear that disappointment awaited me once more.*
>
> *But, no; matters quickly took an unexpected turn. The hunter became the hunted; and instead of either making off or coming for the bait* [a donkey] *prepared for him, the lion began stealthily to stalk me! For about two hours he horrified me by slowly creeping round and round my crazy structure, gradually edging his way nearer and nearer. Every moment I expected him to rush it... I began to feel distinctly "creepy" and heartily repented my folly in having placed myself in such a dangerous position. I kept perfectly still, however, hardly daring even to blink my eyes, but the long continued strain was telling on my nerves.*

The Citizen

September 13, 1994

BIBLE-CLUTCHING MAN MAULED IN LION'S DEN

LONDON – A man was mauled and critically injured by three lions at the London Zoo yesterday after he scaled a 7 metre fence and climbed into their den clutching a bible, zoo officials said. The man, unidentified and in his early 20s, was evacuated by helicopter to a hospital where he was listed in stable but critical condition after emergency surgery for chest injuries. "The lions were holding the unfortunate man," said senior zoo curator Simon Tonge. "One had him by the neck and the two younger ones were biting his legs. He was conscious, he wasn't screaming. I suppose you would say he was writhing on the ground, obviously in some pain," said Mr. Tonge. "There was some blood." "We greatly regret the incursion today and the injuries suffered by this man," said zoo director Jo Gipps. "Security is as tight as is reasonably possible. However, if an individual is sufficiently determined, he or she may succeed in breaching our enclosures."

Patterson then felt a blow behind the head, which terrified him beyond words. Lesser men would have, at this stage, died of a heart attack or yelled for help. But Patterson soon realized it was nothing more harmful than an owl. His involuntary start caused the lion to growl. It now began to advance. "I could barely make out his form... I took careful aim and pulled the trigger. The sound of the shot was at once followed by a most terrific roar, and then I could hear him leaping about in all directions." The lion bounded off, but was not far away when Patterson heard it plunging about. He sent more shots after it and then heard it groan. Gradually the moans became long, deep, sighs and finally even these stopped. The first man-eater of Tsavo was dead, and, as Patterson shouted the news from his *machan*, hundreds of coolies in nearby camps yelled, "*Mabarak! Mabarak!*" (Savior). The lion, although without much mane, was an excellent specimen, measuring nine feet, eight inches from nose to tail tip, and three feet, nine inches at the shoulder.

While the railway from Mombasa to Lake Victoria was under construction, four engineers were housed in a first-class railway car. They had turned two compartments into sleepers, so that both upper and lower berths were in use. Doors and windows were open all night. However, one of the engineers had made up his bed on the platform. In the middle of the night one of the man-eaters appeared, stepped carefully over the snoring man on the platform, climbed up into the corridor, went past the first compartment, the door of which stood open, went into the other, stood up on the man who was lying on the lower berth, seized the poor devil in the upper berth and jumped out the window with him.

Why hunt that man rather than any of the others? Why would a lion step over one or more humans ringed in their sleeping bags around a campfire, sniffing at each one, to single out one individual from all the others? As stated before, I believe that lions can tell the difference between meat and fish eaters. During the Viet Nam War, an instrument in Project Batboy consisted of a gas chromatograph paired with a radio-telemetry unit that could essentially tell the difference between meat-eaters and herbivores by their scent. This ability helped the Americans determine if a group of men were American meat-eaters or Viet Cong fish-eaters. If that is a determinable attribute, can animals have that same skill? In an article

in *Sports Afield*, August 1984, called "Scent of the Carnivore," Lanbourne Rust asks if animals smell different because of their diets. Would vegetarian prey smell less threatening and therefore be less trouble subduing to a predator, than a potentially difficult meat-eater? Alligators on a fish diet are much less aggressive than those on a meat diet. When they change to meat they grow much faster and larger...and more aggressive.

There were periods of some weeks when the workers were not attacked, but that was only because the lions were raiding surrounding villages. Patterson was constantly amazed at how even stronger *bomas* were penetrated by the lions and without a sound. He was also amazed at their cunning. At one point, when they were trying to trap the lions in a double cage, two shooters were used to lure the lions, along with other bait. But they were safe, armed, and with plenty of ammunition in their one side of the double cage. One lion came into the other, attached cage. Amazingly, after dozens of shots were fired at point-blank range, poisoned was tried, but the lions either were too smart or just preferred eating people by this time.

Today, both lions are mounted and on display in the Field Museum in Chicago. According to Field Museum staff, in an article in *Natural History*, November 1998, "One of the man-eaters had a broken lower right canine with an exposed root; asymmetrical growth of the skull in response to this abnormality suggests the beast had suffered from this condition for a long time. Perhaps he was too disabled to hunt and consume the usual prey. We do know that after he was shot, no more humans were killed, although the second lion made several unsuccessful attacks before being shot as well three weeks later. This suggests that the first lion may have been the main culprit." Both lions had very little mane, unlike the Hollywood film version. The mounted specimens bear only the trace of a mane on their chests and sideburns. This is not uncommon among male lions in the Tsavo region. The explanation for this condition may be either environmental or genetic (see the Mane section of this book).

George Rushby, an East African government official, eliminated the Njombe man-eaters in 1947. They were slightly smaller than most lions, and their pelts were "glossier and more luxuriant than those of lean, hard-working, game-hunting lions." The lions,

Mercury Correspondent
August 21, 1984
LIONS BLAMED FOR MAN'S GRISLY DEATH

JOHANNESBURG — A pride of lions is thought to have eaten a man who fell asleep under a tree, leaving only his skull and thigh bones behind, it was revealed yesterday. The lions still roam the Transvaal Lowveld after the remains of an unidentified man were found under a tree on Dundee Farm, about 20 km from Hoedspruit, last week. "The blood was still fresh and there were lots of lion tracks around the skull and thigh bones," Capt. F.J. le Grange, station commander of Hoedspruit police, said yesterday. Capt. le Grange said nature conservation officers had inspected the death scene and were convinced that a pride of lions had been responsible.

referred to in some records as the "Ubena man-eaters," operated over an area of fifty miles by thirty, in the vicinity of the northern tip of Lake Nyasa (a bit west of Njombe). They first made an appearance in 1932, and by the beginning of World War II were moving about in three or four small prides. In the small game area under Rushby's administration, they killed ninety-six people in 1941, sixty-seven more in 1942, and then another eighty-six confirmed. During this period, they were killing at a heavier rate in a second area and at a lower rate in a third. The renowned man-eaters of Tsavo were amateurs in comparison. Rushby states that rinderpest killed off game and cattle, and the human population starved. The human dead were left in the bush and this was the reason the lions developed a taste for easily acquired human meat. Within a year of this outbreak, there were eighty dead and more than a half-dozen man-eaters on the prowl. Man-eaters leave little behind unless they are really harried. When the victim is a child, the lion usually eats all except the skullcap, which is licked clean. All other bones are usually eaten. In the case of adults, the lion usually leaves the skull and jaws (because of the teeth), the soles of the feet or boots (often with the feet still in them), and bones such as femurs and the hips. The meat is licked off these larger bones by the cat's rasp-like tongue.

Rushby was transferred to Mbeya in the southern province of Tanzania in 1946, and almost immediately received a telegram from W. Wenban-Smith, the Njombe District Commissioner. It read: "I beg you to apply earliest attention to man-eaters. Conditions in this district pathetic." Along the short Njombe section of the Great North Road, seventeen road workers had been eaten. The villages had evolved a "negative form of defense" by drawing into larger communities and abandoning the smaller villages. But the human toll did not decline and, incredibly, during the fourteen years of man-eating, not a single lion had ever been shot in the Njombe area.

Why did it go on for so long a period of time? One possibility is superstition. Some natives in Africa are so completely terrified that, should a parent lose a child during the night to a man-eater, neither mother nor father would dream of mentioning the fact to even a close friend, for fear that the simple invocation of the man-eaters by name would suffice to place the speaker next on the list.

The first thing Rushby discovered, upon reconnoitering the Buhoro Flats on both sides of the Great North Road, was that, except for the White Road supervisor, all of whose workers had been eaten, nobody else would even mention the existence of the man-eaters, so terrified of retribution was the entire surviving populace.

A typical Njombe incident occurred in Rujewa. A lion rushed into the village, bowling people over as it went, and grabbed a woman as her husband stood frozen from shock. Without apparent effort, it carried her in its jaws to a group of lions waiting on the perimeter of the village. They ate the woman in a thicket. The husband, armed with an antique rifle, was one of the few brave enough to go after the lions, but as the party drew near the thicket he came face to face with a lioness. It was carrying his wife's leg. He was so shaken that he could not fire and the lioness walked off.

Rushby had his first opportunity when a messenger brought news that lions had attacked the village of Mambego, fifty miles from where he had anticipated their striking. Two villagers had been taken. Rushby, tired from three futile hunts, raced to Mambego and tracked a lioness, which he shot with four bullets. She did not necessarily need four bullets; it was just that he thought this one "had to be dead." Three more man-eaters were bagged soon after, but the toll of human life did not appear to drop. Nevertheless, the four dead man-eaters encouraged tribesmen to take up the hunt and massive hunts began. These had an immediate effect upon the human death toll. It rose. Tribesmen, firing wildly, killed no lions but managed to kill three of their own. By 1947, the lions' toll was falling abruptly in all but one area, where the lions appeared to be making one last stand. Rushby, splitting his best helpers into pairs, combed the bush and shot a male and female. It seemed to be all over, but when another woman was eaten, two more lionesses were flushed out and shot. Rushby had tried every ruse imaginable to kill the lions but each one failed, including a series of cunning traps. He realized the importance of quick success, because of the already strong tribal superstitions. The problem with traps was that they had to be set with the bait the lions liked best: human meat. But the remains of the tribesmen were scant, since the lions would wander off a dozen miles in any direction by the next day.

Two Lions, Oil on Canvas

All in all, fifteen confirmed man-eaters were shot in Njombe district, two were injured (probably mortally) and five other lions — probably not man-eaters — were killed. Those man-eaters had been responsible for what Rushby describes as, "without doubt the greatest and most sustained record of man-eating ever known in Africa." The hunt lasted fifteen months. In a period of fifteen years, successive generations of killers had eaten an astonishing number of victims — between 1,000 and 1,500 people – the equivalent of an entire village. At the end, George Rushby's scouts killed two lionesses, almost surely the last of their man-eating kind.

These rather gory stories are not the type one sees on television nature programs. In all fairness, the average tourist sees usually well-fed lions in game parks from safe, enclosed vehicles. Most of the lions they see are very quiet animals sleeping off last night's meal. This is not how the average African sees lions. He encounters them while on foot as he travels from village to farm to village. He walks through areas where lions are looking for prey. His odds of encountering nasty lions are much greater than the average photo tourist and he is very vulnerable. Mother Nature indeed has her own order. Then again, one can at times identify with Don Zaidle's belief that "Mother Nature is a cruel, calculating old bitch who will kill you given half the chance."

OTHER MAN-EATERS

I include, for the reader, the following comments on other man-eaters as a brief comparison with lions. Hyenas, leopards, tigers, pumas, bears, wolves, alligators, crocodiles, dogs, and others, and yes, even humans, have practiced man-eating and it is interesting to look at their motivations and impact.

HYENAS

The general public certainly does not know hyenas as man-eaters. They are carnivores, however, and carnivores eat meat. Humans have meat, and humans are a lot easier to catch than fleet-footed game. In the African sleeping-sickness epidemic of 1908–1909, hyenas quickly found that in many of the huts the inmates were a helpless prey. They grew constantly bolder, haunting these sleeping-sickness camps, and each night entered them, busted into the huts, and carried off and ate the dying people. But

occasionally men in full vigor were attacked. Hyenas seized native hunters as they slept beside campfires. A white man by the name of Balestra killed two big man-eating hyenas that had ingested the village idiot of the Mlanje District of Malawi back in 1955. There were between forty and sixty people eaten by the Mlanje hyenas up to 1961. Most were eaten during the warm months, when people were sleeping outside. The hyenas ate everything but the victim's clothes.

LEOPARDS

Leopards are very good at killing. Of all the big cats they are probably the most cunning hunters, so it is not surprising that they are into the man-eating business. At the turn of the last century, the Mirso leopard killed more than a hundred people in the Golis Mountains of Africa. In 1937, the Chambisi man-eater was killed on the spear of its sixty-eighth victim. Of all the man-killing animals, some leopards have the curious habit of not eating any part of their human victims. They just want to kill them. On Tanzania's Ruvuma River, a leopard killed twenty-three people from Masaguru village before Brian Nicholson shot it feeding on the body of a dead elephant. It had not eaten a bit of its human kills. In the Luangwa Valley of Zambia, a leopard bit the throats out of his victims without ever feeding upon them. Nevertheless most leopards kill to eat and there are plenty of man-*eating* leopards to justify the comments here. When a leopard kills a human it could be the only human it will ever kill and eat, or it could be the beginning of a spree that could well run into the hundreds – yes, *hundreds*.

Most accounts of man-eating leopards come from India, where better records are kept and local governments are more structured. In Africa, when an African native disappeared in the bush it could be attributed to any number of causes, and was seldom reported to any central authority anyway. Many African natives of whom one hears nothing are killed in the bush and on lonely paths. In these cases the bodies are probably eaten. But of the majority of man-killing by leopards close to villages, there is little chance of their being allowed to make a meal of their victim unmolested. The villagers must do something to kill the leopard or drive it away. Until recently, there was little known of such incidents. Most of the man-

The Natal Witness

December 17, 1985

NATAL KILLER LIONS SHOT

Two lions that attacked and ate game guard Lance Corporal Mhlupbeki Hlabisa (50) in Hluhluwe game reserve on Saturday have been shot dead by rangers. Rangers hunting the man-eaters sat up all night at baited traps and shot the pair which were lured to the traps sometime on Sunday night or Monday morning, said Natal Parks Board PRO June Payn yesterday. Lions that have tasted people are more likely to do it again. Mr. Hlabisa was killed in a highly unusual chain of events when his horse was charged by a white rhino on Saturday. Avoiding the rhino, he rode into the pride, was thrown from his frightened horse and eaten.

Lilac Breasted Roller, Oil on Canvas

eating leopard data that we have comes from the famous hunter, Jim Corbett. He is acknowledged for with killing more man-eaters (leopards and tigers) in India than anyone.

The Panar leopard of India, for example, is credited with four hundred victims. Corbett thought these numbers were low. He says the inaccuracy of the numbers of victims was because no government bulletins were issued or records kept between April and September of that particular year. Obviously the leopard did not fast during the five months that the government wasn't recording. The Rudraprayag leopard had 125 certified kills.

Siggins calculated the number of deaths caused by leopards in the Medo District between the years 1910 and the First World War at more than seven hundred from one village alone. This includes both visitors and passing natives whose bodies were recovered. He describes two leopards that killed five men and two women in one night on a kopje, an out-cropping of large rocks, at N'koribo.

Corbett maintained that any human kill that took place at night was the work of a leopard, and in daylight that of a tiger. This is disputed in some circles but is probably a reasonable yardstick. Almost all of his experience was in Asia. Although he later moved to Kenya, he had little chance there to hunt man-eaters of any kind. His comparison of Indian leopards and tigers to African lions and leopards would have been fascinating reading.

TIGERS

Almost all of Corbett's man-eating tigers had been either injured by man or were suffering from porcupine-quill damage that had so badly crippled and disabled them that the hunting of normal prey was impossible. But all big cats are opportunists and like most other animals will take advantage of any surplus of food. Much of the man-eating done in India followed the great influenza epidemic of 1918 when there was a large surplus of human flesh. The Champawat tigress did her man-eating in Nepal during this period and in the foothills of Himalayan India. This man-eater is credited with eating 436 people!

Like lions, tigers do not have a reputation for climbing. But, also like lions, they are eminently capable of it. There are many instances of tigers climbing straight up tree trunks, and of hunted

Tigertail, Oil on Canvas

The Natal Witness
September 2, 1994
BOY FLOWN TO CITY AFTER LION ATTACK
A little boy was flown into the city yesterday for treatment at Grey's Hospital after being mauled by a lion in Gabarone, Botswana on Sunday. According to the boy's mother Vicky Wood, Tyrone (4) put his hands through the bars of a lion cage during a visit to a lion park. A full grown female lion mauled his arms.

Nightcrawler, Oil on Canvas

tigers leaping on elephants to get at the *mahout* elephant riders, and sport hunters. According to Roger Caras, nature authority for ABC televison at the time, 275 people were taken by tigers between 1961 and 1971 in the Sundarbans, and at least five lives were taken during the month of April 1973, when the local people were gathering honey. This carnage was dramatically reduced when the government introduced masks with a face that people could wear at the back of their heads. Apparently, the tigers like sneaking up on their prey from the rear.

In Russia, in the remote wilds of the taiga, the Siberian tiger to this day instills a traditional terror in the local residents. In the past, it was a custom of the Cossacks to lash criminals to certain trees in what obviously was a pretty gruesome death sentence. Siberian tigers were familiar with the trees and ate the offenders, probably developing regrettable manners in the meanwhile. In very severe winters, when normal prey may be scarce, these tigers will rob freshly dug graves.

PUMAS

Here in this country at the beginning of the new millennium, we are creating a very similar scenario with our "lion," the mountain lion, cougar, or puma. There are more and more reports of campers, joggers, and hunters being attacked and sometimes killed by this American lion. In California alone, man-puma confrontations are increasing at an enormous rate. In the early nineties, puma hunting was banned. As a consequence, the cat proliferated and, driven out by its parents, started expanding its territory. But so were the human developments. Residential areas are expanding further into the foothills and the puma's previously wild hunting territory. This is not only taking normal habitat away from them but it is decimating the cat's normal prey. Guess what? The puma sees very little deer but does see the more plentiful joggers and hikers that are certainly much easier to catch than a running deer. Sound familiar? In 1994 alone, California had more than three hundred serious attacks by pumas on humans, including two fatalities.

When he was an ecologist with the University of California at Berkeley, Paul Beier did a study that documented fifty-seven puma attacks on man from the turn of the century to 1990 in the U.S., with ten of them fatal. That is ten dead in ninety years. Since 1990, however, Don Zaidle, in his book *American Man-Killers*, reports a total of fourteen deaths officially attributed to lion predation in North America. That is fourteen dead people in only six recent years. He presents a good case for presuming that the number of people killed in puma attacks that we do not know about probably exceeds those that we do. Just four of the twelve states with large lion populations show 130 recent, officially recorded attacks. Well over two-thirds occurred in the 1990s alone. Extrapolating from these figures, a national tally of several hundred to possibly more than a thousand attacks by these normally shy animals does not seem unreasonable in the very near future.

In Montclair, California, police killed a lion when it advanced toward them after being shot with a tranquilizer dart on the loading dock of the J.C. Penney store in the town's shopping mall. At another mall, terrified shoppers competed with a cougar for parking space as it prowled the lot. It took refuge under a car after being darted. Zaidle reports dogs being taken literally off the leash while they were walked. One man killed a lion on his living room rug after it chased his pet dachshund inside. Wildlife researchers have documented lions giving birth beneath porches of homes within the city limits of Boulder, Colorado. Many people reported missing in puma country could well be victims of these cats. Zaidle says that four adults missing in just one southern California county are believed to be lion victims but are not counted in the statistics.

Expansion by young cougars looking for their own territory brings them into urban areas. Sixty percent of recent human attacks are by young pumas. In 1987, California's Casper Park authorities thought that one area of the park was so potentially dangerous that no one under age eighteen was allowed in. Peter Capstick told me of finding a set of cougar tracks in a golf-course sand trap near his home in Naples, Florida. An article about puma incidents in the *Star Ledger* (Newark, New Jersey) November 29, 2002, gives more reason for concern. It points out that there is a very marked increase of attacks on people, which now average about four times as many per year than in 1970. It stated, in contrast to other estimates, that since 1890, mountain lions have killed seventeen people, eleven of them children, in the United

October 18, 1993
LION ATTACK
DAR ES SALAAM — Two villagers in Tanzania's southern coastal region of Lindi were killed and three others badly injured in an attack by a man-eating lion last week, according to reports reaching here Saturday. The reports said that in the first attack on the Mji Mwema village, the lion killed an old woman at night after she left her hut.

Midnight Express, Oil on Canvas

States and Canada. More than half of these deaths occurred in just the past twelve years.

More remarkable is how the cat is being driven further eastward. A car killed a juvenile male cougar (puma) in 2002 on Interstate 35 near Kansas City. They hadn't had a confirmed sighting of a free-roaming mountain lion in that region in more than 100 years. In Michigan, scientists have confirmed the presence of seven mountain lions in northern Michigan where they had supposedly been wiped out ninety-five years ago, but their existence in the state is still debated.

As pointed out before, California and Colorado especially have the more immediate problem. In 1991 near the city of Colorado Springs, an eighteen year-old man was killed while jogging at mid-day about 200 yards from a high school. This was the first adult to be killed and consumed by a healthy full-grown lion in that area in at least 100 years. Man-eating by pumas is not common but will probably rise as more confrontations create more opportunities for them to develop a taste for us. Since then, many public officials have feared that the next death could happen at any time. Pete Taylor, lead ranger for the Open Space and Mountain Parks Department in Boulder, thinks so too. "I think it is going to happen in town," said Taylor, who responds to mountain lion sightings in parks and backyards nearly every month. "It took me eight and a half years to see five lions in Boulder. I have seen six in the last eighteen months. We are either getting more lions or the lions are getting more used to us."

They do get around. Young male mountain lions have been observed traveling 400 miles to establish new territory. Nearly all of these lions are forced to find new turf. Those that do not travel tend to be killed and eaten by their territorial elders, a very good incentive for leaving.

Incidents were and are very rare where these predators are hunted and indeed were rare in these very same areas when they were previously hunted. Hunted animals (whether with bullets or non-lethal stun weapons) have a healthy respect for man and deliberately keep away from him.

When these animals were hunted they would never come near man much less travel into developed areas. That is precisely why the pumas have gotten bolder.

BEARS

Bears are big and well-equipped killers. Add that to their unpredictability and you have one animal that demands a hell of a lot of respect. Or, as Alaskan Steve Augustin says, "Anything that flips over three-hundred-pound boulders to lick bugs off the bottom is nothing to take lightly." Bear maulings occur throughout the state of Alaska and involve every kind of bear — black, brown, grizzly, and polar. Most bear attacks come from just being in the bear's way, especially if it has no other direction to go. These attacks are much more serious when a sow and cubs are involved, or when the bear is on a kill. Bear attacks on hunters, of course, are understandable, but there are so many documented cases of hikers, campers, photographers, scientists, and non-hunters in general, that bears should be a major concern if you are in their country.

When I was fishing at Bob Devito's fishing camp in Alaska in the early eighties, he told me of a bear that chased him on to the porch of the main cabin, where he finally had to shoot it or lose clients one way or the other. Bud Branham, one of the premier Alaskan guides, told me that most of the time the bear just wants to avoid humans. But if you spend a great deal of time in their domain, it is only a matter of time before those percentages change, favoring an ugly confrontation. Dr. Stephen Herrero, animal-behavior specialist with the University of Calgary, Alberta, analyzed 279 grizzly encounters resulting in 165 injuries, including nineteen deaths. He also reports that more than five hundred people were injured by black bears between 1960 and 1980 in North America. It seems that most grizzly attacks on humans by sows are to protect cubs. Assuming defensive positions like placing your hands over your neck while in a fetal position on the ground help show you are not a threat. She will probably leave you alive after tearing you up a bit. Boars, on the other hand, usually attack because they want to eat you.

Some of the stories here are from the books of Larry Kaniut. His *Alaska Bear Tales*, and its sequel, *More Alaska Bear Tales*, deal strictly with Alaska incidents. In them he cites 152 grizzly maulings, forty-four of them fatal, between 1900 and 1989, overlapping with Dr. Herrero's in only a few instances. Their combined numbers yield 317 attacks resulting in injury. It is required read-

The Pretoria News
May 10, 1994
NELSPRUIT — A man has been killed by a lion in the Kruger National Park. The police in the Eastern Transvaal said tourists had seen a lion eating human remains next to a dirt road between the Letaba and Olifants camps in the north of the park. A game warden investigated the report, and the lioness dragged the remains to a rocky outcrop. She was shot. Footprints belonging to four people were seen in the area. The police are investigating.

Above Brooks Lake, Oil on Canvas

ing for the outdoorsman in bear country who wants to know how to handle bear confrontations.

There have been an average of two people mauled each year in Alaska in the last nine decades. According to Kaniut, roughly a quarter of those victims died. The greatest danger was to a person traveling alone. Although a recent fatality involved a bear that attacked a search party of seven, there is usually safety in numbers. Eighteen percent of those attacked in the woods were rescued by a partner, while 2.7 percent were saved by a dog. Nearly 9 percent lived by feigning death, with the bear leaving.

Mike Dishnow, an educator from Wasilla, Alaska, was doing graduate work at the University of Alaska in Anchorage. He was staying at the Quartz Creek campground with his wife and one-year-old son, Mickey, on the Kenai Peninsula during the summer of 1978. The first night in camp, a bear tore through the rain fly and the wall of the tent. "We froze for what must have been minutes, but seemed like hours," said Dishnow. Just as abruptly, the bear left. "We ran to the truck. Ruth became hysterical and broke down crying. I was shaky and could see myself trembling as I took down the tent. My wife has not been in a tent since."

Chris Thompson, a former police officer, lived in Anchorage. In the spring of 1987, he and his friend, Doug, went fishing on Grant Creek, near Moose Pass, about forty-five miles southeast of Hope. When fly-fishing, they became separated. While taking a fly out of a tree, Thompson heard a noise in the brush and saw a large brown object hurling towards him from about forty or fifty yards away. He dropped the fishing rod and instinctively drew his pistol out of his holster. The bear was instantly in front of him.

I had my handgun cocked and was aiming right at his head. The bear made a woofing sound. He was so close to me that I could actually see the pink in his lips when he barked. He stood there for ten or fifteen seconds, lifting his nose up in the air, trying to smell me. The bear woofed another time or two, but I held my ground with my handgun cocked and aimed. He began walking away, taking four or five steps at a time and then looking back over his shoulder at me. I still held my ground until he was out of sight, then backed down the hill toward my buddy. Doug holstered his .44, which he had also drawn when he saw the bear. Once I had crossed the creek, we hurried back to our car as if the bear was following us all the way. There really aren't words to describe the fear inside you when you're facing a bear at that close range, staring into his eyes, trying to guess his next move. I had worked as a police officer for eight years, so I drew my weapon naturally, without even realizing it. I remember looking down the barrel, into the sights and noticing that I wasn't even shaking. But after that bear turned and walked away, I couldn't have held a cup of coffee if I had tried.

Don Zaidle in his book *American Man-Killers*, along with Dr. Herrero, believes that 317 confirmed grizzly attacks resulting in injuries, with sixty-three deaths, is less than half the true amount.

Zaidle's book is loaded with stories of interesting encounters, from the bear that ate a family's Christmas dinner after chasing them out of their cabin, then fell asleep on the floor, to many with more tragic encounters. Two of these fatal incidents occurred simultaneously. On the night of August 13, 1967, two different bears attacked two groups of campers about an hour apart, and about 45 miles from each other, in Glacier National Park. Both of those killed and eaten were girls, both were nineteen years old.

Don points out that in this country, man-eating by bears and other predators is almost always portrayed as an aberration. No one ever suggests the possibility that the bears were simply hungry. Jim Rearden, a former U.S. Fish & Wildlife field agent who has studied and written about bears for years, flatly states in his

The Pretoria News
October 6, 1992
9 YEAR OLD GIRL EATEN BY LION
GABARONE — A 9-year-old girl was last week dragged from a camp-fire and devoured by a lion in the north-western part of the country. Atweng Galebotswe had been camping with her family at Chao Island. The girl's father, Mr. Keraetswe Galebotswe, said the lioness grabbed Atweng and dragged her for about 15 m before it started devouring her. "We attacked the lion with sticks, but it pulled my child into the bushes." The Botswana Defence Force later shot the lioness.

book *Tales of Alaska's Big Bears*, "Bears attack humans because they are hungry." Likewise, Herrero observes that "bears may prey on campers during the night." One of the most recent examples of this occurred on October 9, 1995, when two British Columbia hunters, Shane Fumerton and William Caspell, were killed by a bear that wanted their elk meat. Both men carried heavy rifles, and at least one of them had a round chambered and ready to fire, yet it happened so quickly that neither had time to get off a shot. As Don points out, the leap from associating humans with food to viewing them as food is not a very big one.

And no, you cannot outrun a grizzly: Its speed is estimated at up to forty miles an hour in a short sprint. As an old trapper once added, it might be a good idea however to be able to out-run your campmates.

In my own area of New Jersey we see bears much too frequently for a residential area. We saw a small one in my neighbor's driveway and a two hundred and fifty-pounder was killed by a car a couple of years ago just four hundred yards from here. And I live only an hour from Broadway and Lincoln Center! Just last month a child was taken out of its carriage and killed by a black bear in a *shopping center* in the lower part of New York, about thirty-five miles from where I live.

If nothing is done about making these animals have a healthy respect for people there are going to be a lot more incidents in residential areas.

WOLVES

In the course of researching the text for this book, I have come across some very surprising things. None of these amazed me more than the man-eating done by wolves. I had always been under the impression that man-eating by wolves was only a historical thing — that it happened before the age of the firearm, and very seldom since. If you also thought that, hold on to your hats!

First, let me establish that these are man-eating wolves of Eurasia and not North America. The Eurasian wolves have one hell of a track record of human depredation, whereas it is very difficult to pin down a genuine case of man-eating in North America, let alone a determined attack. With the rare instances caused by injury or provocation, man-eating by wolves in this hemisphere is almost non-existent. That even includes accounts from Native American lore. Nowhere is there a tradition of man-eating by wolves among any of the American tribes, and wolves were all over the place when the bison roamed America. There are plenty of reports of wolf attacks by settlers, but these were mostly related to livestock confrontations and interpreted by those settlers who were immigrants from Europe.

In Eurasia, however, wolves, even since World War II, have a long history of eating people.

France has a rich heritage of wolf incidents. From old parish records in Abbé François Fabré, a man-eating wolf ate sixty-four people and attacked another ninety-seven. There is confusion about whether this wolf may have had an accomplice. Nevertheless, a sixty-year-old farmer killed the man-eater of Gevaudan on June 19, 1766. A schoolteacher was eaten in her own classroom in 1900. The last reported death in that country was in Dordogne, in 1914. The victim was an eight-year-old girl eaten near her house. The wolf is probably no longer found in France.

Spain has always had wolves and still does in the wilder areas. Italy also has viable wolf packs, including recent man-killers. In 1956, a postman was killed and eaten in an area about two hour's drive from Rome. Six years earlier, a soldier was torn apart by wolves after defending himself with his bayonet, killing one wolf before the rest got him.

The Russian steppes and taiga have always had wolves, and man-eating wolves have never been rare. Peter the Great used to have a unique winter sleigh ride. He and his guests would gallop through the Russian night dragging a squealing piglet. This commotion attracted wolves that then gave chase. The wolves would eventually reach the tiring horses. At the critical moment, the hapless piglet would be cut loose and left in the midst of the frenzied wolves. The trick apparently was to distract the wolves just enough to give the horses time to turn around and get enough lead to make it home before the wolves caught up with them again. According to James Clarke, the village of Pilovo was decimated by a concerted wolf attack during a food shortage in 1927. The survivors were eventually rescued by the army. Pollard tells of a cara-

Serious Business, Oil on Canvas

van being completely wiped out by man-eating wolves in the Ural Mountains around 1914.

World War II was responsible for a tremendous increase in the wolf population of Europe. The glut of abandoned corpses in the wilder places ensured that even the weakest of cubs would survive. The predation must have been enormous after the many German-Russian battles. Humans became the wolves' main diet. The Russians reported 30,000 wolves shot in a single year in the 1960s and more than 70,000 assorted barnyard animals killed by them, plus eleven people eaten out of 168 reported attacks on man.

By 1949, Finland was having such a problem that it mounted a campaign against wolves, which were eating both stock and people. Despite the use of aircraft and machine-guns, only a few wolves were killed; the rest came back out of the deep forest as soon as the pressure was off.

Eleven children were eaten by wolves in Portugal in 1945. In ten years up to 1955, there were just short of 7,000 wolves killed in southern Yugoslavia.

There seems to be no other important differences between the wolves of North America and those of Eurasia, but what a difference.

ALLIGATORS AND CROCODILES

Officially, there were no fatal American alligator attacks on humans before 1973. The Florida Game and Fresh Water Fish Commission is the only agency with records of alligator attacks. Their strict rules accepted only human evidence that was actually in the alligators' stomachs. A nine-year-old boy found mauled in 1957 in Brevard County was ruled ineligible on the basis that he had drowned before the gators got him. But consider this: Alligators kill terrestrial prey *by* drowning them, and death from secondary causes, such as blood loss or a broken neck, is purely coincidental. Indigestible material is apparently retained indefinitely, not passed in the usual manner. Human jewelry is a staple item in the stomachs of man-eating African crocs, and dog collars show up fairly regularly in American alligators, sometimes with readable dates on vaccination tags that show them to be quite old.

In the United States Department of Agriculture Technical Bulletin No. 147, *The Habits and Economic Importance of Alligators,* December 1929, by Dr. Remington Kellog, Assistant Curator of Mammals, United States National Museum, Kellog mentions no fewer than twelve attacks, seven of them fatal, and alludes to additional reports appearing "in the press from time to time of attacks on persons by alligators."

A group of salt-water crocs is reliably reported to have killed and eaten nearly a thousand men at a single sitting, and in just one night! It happened during World War II on Ramree Island, just off the Burma Coast. Bruce Wright, a naturalist and member of the British forces at the time, describes the event in *Crocodiles and Alligators,* from aboard a launch grounded in the swamp.

> *The scattered rifle shots in the pitch black swamp punctured by the screams of wounded men crushed in the jaws of huge reptiles, and the blurred worrying sound of spinning crocodiles made a cacophony of hell that has rarely been duplicated on earth. At dawn the vultures arrived to clean up what the crocodiles had left...Of about one thousand Japanese that entered the swamps of Ramree, only about twenty were found alive.*

Louisianians Ted Joanen and Larry McNease, in a report on alligator farming practices, note that the behavior of alligators fed on fish and meat showed obvious differences. They found that animals fed fish were shy and wary, whereas those fed the meat of nutria, a large rodent, were aggressive and generally more active. Diet was also "found to have a significant impact on productivity."

As far as size goes, alligators and crocodiles can be a force to be reckoned with. Don Zaidle says that, according to Louisiana records, "two Nimitz-class swamp-cruisers collected in 1718 measured nineteen and twenty-two feet respectively, and probably weighed close to a ton each." Twenty feet is huge for even a Nile crocodile let alone an American alligator. Nevertheless, a 'gator killed in 1879 near Avery island, Louisiana, measured eighteen feet, five inches, and another, nineteen feet, two inches, was killed in 1890. In 1956, one measuring seventeen feet, five inches, was

Fritz's Hippo, Oil on Canvas

killed in Lake Apoptka. Zaidle says that slightly less than 2,500 complaints about alligators were reported in 1982, but over the summer of 1995, Florida wildlife authorities had 12,000 incidents. Florida's gators are becoming less afraid of man. Downplaying of assaults by alligators seems to prevail in Florida. Bad for the "snow bird" business, I guess. Most of the fatalities caused by these huge reptiles occur in third-world countries. We in America usually see an alligator in golf-course-type situations, not ambushing a boatman in New Guinea or a water bearer at an African river.

DOGS

Although they aren't man-eaters, according to a report in the September 1989 issue of the *Journal of the American Medical Association,* 183 people were killed by dogs in the ten years leading up to 1988, most of them children, which is nearly double the acknowledged deaths by alligators, bears, and cougars combined, and in just ten years! Dogs kill an average of approximately ten people per year in this country.

HUMANS

Oh, yes, people are still very much a factor in man-eating. During the Congo uprisings of the 1960s it was common practice in northeastern Congo for opponents to eat each other's heart and liver, as soon as possible after they had been killed, so as to gain their strength. Near Lake Bilibizi, a tribe practiced cannibalism. A.J. Siggins said that often people were murdered so that they could enjoy a feast of "long pig."

> *Those who have eaten human flesh say that it has a sweet flavour, comparable, though less coarse, to that of young donkeys or zebras and not unlike pork, although I have read the meat tastes like veal, only sweeter. I found cannibals and part of a human thighbone in a big pot close to my camp at Navanka in the Lomwe country. I have never tasted human flesh myself but knew*

> *two sailors who had been forced to eat one of their companions when cast adrift in an open boat and they told me it was a nauseous meal, I imagine it tastes somewhat similar to monkey, which I have eaten, but have no wish to pry further into the question.*

CAMPFIRE CHATTER

My favorite time on the many trips I've taken is evening around the campfire. Whether on the plains of Africa, the mountains of Alaska, or the trout streams of the Rockies, there is a wonderful finish to the day's events when by the campfire. Starting with sundowners and ending with whatever may be left at two in the morning, the gathering at a campfire has a magic all its own. The crowd may be skiers, biologists, hunters, or fishermen, or it may just be a gathering of one's self during a solitary evening. The campfire is the dessert of the day's meal, to be savored and cherished like a vintage port. I wonder at so many people who have their outdoor grills and patios, but not a fire pit. We have one, and it is probably the most popular place at our home. It certainly is with the children. Whether warming the snow of January or smoking out the mosquitoes of July, our children love an outdoor fire. I am a child myself, when it comes to enjoying the hypnotic flames of a campfire.

The conversation at African campfires usually revolves around the experiences of African bush veterans, as told to their fascinated clients or guests. One of the most frequently asked questions is, "What is the most dangerous of the African game?" We are spellbound when we hear all sorts of stories, most of which are from the narrator's personal experiences. We think of the "big five": lion, leopard, Cape buffalo, elephant, and rhino. We are surprised to find that the answer depends on so many other things. "Kalahari lions are more aggressive than those of East Africa." "Kenyan buffalo are nastier than those in the south." Is the encounter a surprise encounter or not? Is the animal wounded or not? If a predator, is it starving or not? We may completely forget that the crocodile takes a lot of villagers at rivers but we don't hear as much

Joe's Lion, Oil on Canvas

about them. And no experienced African wants to be between water and a cranky hippo. Many of the professional hunters in East Africa ranked a wounded buffalo as more dangerous than any other animal, probably because they are so determined and so tough. Just as many will cite the wounded lion because, after all, killing is his livelihood, and he is very good at it. Others cite the wounded leopard that will get at anyone he wants, but prefers not to hang around long enough to finish the job. In recent years, the protection of elephants is enlarging their herds again. These nomadic giants are killing more and more farmers and humans in general as they roam into the ever-expanding human populations.

Many of my trips to Africa have been with art collectors who hunt, while others have been solitary trips for photographic or scientific purposes. All of these opinions are gathered from professional tour guides, biologists, and hunters, many of whom are a living bridge between the old, wild, and woolly days between the two World Wars, and the present. They still refer to the wars in Kenya as "The Kaiser's War" and "The Hitler War."

I hope you will bear with me as I share some of the things I have seen and learned:

I have been very fortunate to witness the yearly wildebeest migration in East Africa. As far as I could see, the plains were a moving mass of animals, mostly wildebeest and zebra. It is a truly awesome yet humbling experience. Much of the game concentrations left today are a direct result of the terrible tsetse fly. It was deadly to domestic cattle, and the infested areas became open for game animals, which fortunately were immune to their bites. The sleeping sickness these flies carry is deadly to humans, and took a very high toll. Mind you, sleeping sickness or not, tsetse fly bites are nothing to shrug off. I swear the damn things bite before they even land on you. One of the areas where I camped often was on the Chobe river or Linyanti swamp at a place called camp Saile. These areas were full of tsetse flies, which was why they were so great for game. In those days the "john" was up on a huge anthill. It was not uncommon to find mambas or cobras, and I can tell you it was quite a decision to go up there at night if you had forgotten your flashlight, which I often did.

It was at a campfire at Saile that John Dugmore, a third-generation, ex-hunter, and native of Kenya and Zimbabwe, told me that if a Cape buffalo charges, all you need to do is drop to the ground. He will then jump over you. Knowing buffalo enough to think he was kidding me, I questioned him. Unbelievably, I found that as a teenager he and his friends used to hunt buffalo with the Africans, using spears and dogs. If the surrounded buffalo came your way in order to escape the spears and the dogs nipping at his heels, you simply dropped to let him jump over you. Trust me. Don't try it.

I also learned why such a giant animal as the elephant can move so quietly on his huge padded feet. If not for the rumblings of his ever-working stomach, he wouldn't be heard even when passing just a few yards away. Yet at Pom-Pom camp in the Okavango, in September 1998, we and our friends Lorraine and Rich McGinn could get no sleep because of the racket raised by elephants tearing down trees directly over our tents. The elephants sent all kinds of debris bouncing off our tent's roofs. There was no sleeping that night. The McGinns were great sports about it all. It was their first African safari.

Pat Hepburn, a Botswana citizen and professional guide before his death, told me of (and displayed his fondness for) eating the flying termites that come out after an Okavango rain, which taste like soft gooey cashews (yes, I had been drinking.) He explained that in his beloved Kalahari, the dry temperatures could change as much as 55 degrees in a twenty-four hour period, reaching well over a hundred degrees while still in the shade.

I learned that a tourist hunter will pay thousands of dollars for a license to shoot a male lion, leopard or elephant. But in order to qualify for a license he must also pay twenty or thirty thousand dollars for a three to four-week safari. An elephant or lion hunt in total can cost forty to sixty thousand dollars. Hunters bring in more foreign exchange than most people realize. Hunting income is a great incentive for African governments to protect their wildlife from extinction. I learned that, under the right circumstances, one can be more concerned about the carnivorous safari ants than lions, that you can always find water near yellow fever trees, and that

The Citizen
July 29, 1998
WOMAN MAULED BY LIONS
"OUT ON WALK"
MADRID — Walking pet lions around the neighborhood can be risky. Two lions, a male and female, became agitated while being walked in the southern Spanish town of Cecta early yesterday and mauled four women passers-by, injuring three of them critically, a local official said. A government statement said the lions, which are one and two years old respectively, were being kept illegally in dog houses without proper documentation and would be taken to separate zoos. It did not say what would happen to the unidentified man who was walking them.—Reuters.

Midnight Marauders, Oil on Canvas

rinderpest and tsetse flies are the friends of wildlife because they keep man and his cattle from completely overtaking the wild land.

I saw a video where photographer Mike Penman of Botswana crawls up to lions and they even swat him on the rear. These were wild lions, but he knew them very well. He says they were curious when he didn't run from them. Better you than me, Mike.

Lloyd Wilmot at Lloyd's Camp in Botswana had a tented camp in the Okavango Swamp — with a Corden-Bleu cook, mind you. Apparently there are great cooks that are as pleased to have the African experience as he and his clients were at having their cooking. He was showing me hunting dogs and lions, when one of the resident hyenas came over to inspect us in the vehicle. I saw him actually pet this wild hyena. Very slowly, mind you, but pet it with his bare hand he did. He feels that hyenas are very much misunderstood. I'll take his word for it. When trapped by a breeding herd of elephant, he has also hidden in elephant dung to escape their notice. That same day we were watching such a herd drinking in a pond or pan through some scant brush at the edge of the water. A cheeky little calf came around behind us and started squealing like a stuck pig when the mother discovered us. Lloyd was trying to convince me I should freeze. The next I remember was watching from underneath the truck as the elephants left the pan. I had run the forty yards back and dived under the vehicle. This old artist has used up all the close calls with elephants that anyone is entitled to, thank you very much!

Although insects don't eat people as some animals do, they certainly can make almost as big an impression. Siggins claimed that insects were a much larger problem for the European settlers than were lions, and that the mosquito was the deadliest man-killer in Africa. He describes nights of scorpions and ants. They slept on the ground in those days, "...without tents or mosquito nets, making a bed of grass, first digging a hole for our hip bones and packing it, laying the ground sheet on top and then blankets, with a saddle for a pillow. If it rained we pulled the ground sheet over the top or slept on until the blanket got too sodden for comfort then got up and sat under a tree." Yuck!

There are down-sides to campfires, I am sure, but I just don't want to see them. John Lawrence, the famous Mercedes road-racer and lion hunter from Kenya, did point out an obvious danger on one occasion, however. We were on the Chobe River in northern Botswana, in a camp which was very close to hippos. Lions were always coming into camp and I just thought it all very exciting. The hippo grunting was so close that my cot seemed to vibrate. I hardly sleep when on safari because I'm so keyed up. After dinner the guides go to bed early to get away from tourists. We then sit by the fire telling each other how brave we were earlier that day when this animal charged and that animal got too close. Eventually the rest retire and I try always to be the last to give in to fatigue. This is my time. I spread the glowing coals so there is no longer a bright flame. Now the starlit night is that much easier to see. There is then just the red glow of the coals radiating their warmth...and those mystical sounds of an African night. I am in another state of consciousness. After a few trips to the mess tent for some liquid refreshment I finally retire to my tent. Because I snore so loudly, they always place me in the farthest tent.

One morning John asked me if I enjoyed my visitor the previous night. I told him there was none while I was up. When showed the tracks of a huge lion, I proudly pointed out that the lion tracks were on top of mine — that he came after I had retired. But those were the tracks I made going to the mess tent for refills on my liquid refreshments. John showed me where my tracks going to bed were covering those same lion tracks! He showed me where the lion had stopped to look at me and walked on. He had been only a few yards behind me! On seeing my concern, he simply said that this lion probably didn't like his prey reeking of juniper berries.

On another occasion I was awakened by one of those noises you can't quite describe because it is practically over by the time you awaken. I thought it was a particular camp-mate, who had no shortage of practical jokes, none of which were appreciated. When he didn't respond, I thought it odd and returned to sleep. In the morning we discovered leopard tracks leading right into the entrance of my hut. Because we had mosquito netting I had left the door open the whole night.

There was another incident when the assistant cook was dragged from his tent by a lion. The cook ran out after them beat-

The Miami Herald
October 13, 1982

MOM FIRES AT LION, HITS DAUGHTER

PASADENA, Texas (AP) — A woman accidentally shot her 31-year-old daughter who was struggling with a pet African lioness that had escaped from its cage, authorities said. Connie Shams, the cat's owner, was treated for bites on her legs and a minor gunshot wound on the hand, said police spokesman Mac Craft. The lioness was killed by police officers. "Connie looked out her window and saw that the pet lion was out of her cage. She went out and tried to put it back in, but apparently the lion didn't like the idea and mauled her," Craft said. Shams's mother, Christine Lamb, heard her daughter screaming for help, grabbed a .357 Magnum and fired several times, hitting the lion and striking Shams on the hand. "Thank God I got the gun out," she said. "There wasn't enough time to call the police."

ing pots and pans on the lion that dropped its victim and disappeared into the night. In those days it was all part of the excitement.

Another of my own campfire stories deals with my first real near-death experience, (which more embarrassingly was even recorded on film and shown on all three television networks and at gallery exhibitions). Back in those days the police called it the "death euphoria" — that period of time when bliss takes over and you look forward to ending it all. You feel absolutely wonderful. You feel no pain. Every big and little care and problem you have ever experienced will never again happen. Unfortunately, I have been trying to get into that state through meditation for years, with not much success.

In February 1972, I had a very successful fund-raising auction of two of my paintings for the World Wildlife Fund at the Breakers Hotel in Palm Beach, Florida. Although a particular person directly expressed an interest in my elephant painting, I was surprised when she did not acquire it. Although it certainly was a wild elephant, she told me it was not wild enough. She was a big game huntress and all the ones that she saw were very wild. I was devastated and vowed to solve the problem.

That fall I was on the Zambezi River in Zambia with the express purpose of photographing angry elephants. Although we were in a recently established game park, run by the Wildlife Conservation International, I suppose there is some fear of man in the elephant's collective memory. An ex-professional hunter assured me that if you stand up to a charging elephant it will stop because they are not used to the strange experience of much smaller animals or people challenging them. An imaginary barrier like a log or bush is to be used as a boundry. The elephant is supposed to stay behind. My companion Brick Stang actually showed me how it was done and how exciting it was. We had no firearms. Twice he went up to an elephant and stood his ground as the elephant stopped his charge just ten to twenty feet from him. I was ecstatic. This was really neat!

After this demonstration we had lunch with the game warden, Eric Balson, who had been head of the Tanzania Game Department. He left Tanzania because he unsuccessfully tried to arrest one of the country's leading poachers, President Julius Nyerere's brother.

After lunch with Eric, it was my turn to play with the elephants. After all, I was now an expert on handling them, right? (Eric had warned us not to play around with the elephants but we didn't listen.) We found three elephants on the riverbed and I promptly ran up trying to get them to look aggressive and charge. They very decently tried to ignore me until I started throwing sticks and stones to get their attention. I got it, all right. The smaller one came at me and I stood and actually stepped into its charge. It stopped, trumpeted, tossed its head and dust all around, and retreated. I was so excited I threw my brand new movie camera into the air (and fortunately caught it on the way down). So it went with the other elephants as well. It was awesome.

We had to leave for the vehicle to catch the last dugout ferry across a small river, but I insisted on a few more "takes." I ran up to the last remaining elephant, since the other two were grazing with the rest of the herd a quarter of a mile away. He apparently had enough. He came at me like an express train. Unlike all the elephant charges you see in paintings and photos, with the ears spread out to give a more impressive intimidating look, this one had its ears flat against his neck and head down. I heard someone, yell, "Get the hell out of there!" I threw my movie camera at the elephant as I turned to run. After running what I thought was a reasonable distance, I turned (while still running) to see where it had stopped, only to find its trunk about three feet from my head trying to grab me!

I realized it was all over. I felt a whack on my back from its trunk. I landed on my belly in the sand and completely out of breath. I remember a tsetse fly in my nose and one buzzing in my mouth. I felt the elephant's tusk hit my head twice. His foot kind of wedged me into a slight depression. On turning to look upward all I saw was a sky full of elephant. It was then that I heard a shot. Eric had heard the racket made by the elephants, jumped in his four-wheel-drive and came to the top of the twenty-foot riverbank to investigate. He fired a shot in front of me, which was supposed to scare the pachyderm, but apparently neither one of us heard it. The second shot hit the elephant high in the honeycombed skull of its forehead. The stunned animal spun dizzily

The Pretoria News

September 14, 1983

DAR ES SALAAM— Lions killed and ate two women from the same family in the Lindi district of southern Tanzania last week, says the ruling Revolutionary Party's newspaper *Uhuru*. The newspaper quoted a police commander yesterday as saying the women's deaths brought to 18 the number of people killed by lions in the region this year. — Reuters.

Working Ladies, Oil on Canvas

around with one foot landing between my knee and chest as another brushed my side and neck. It looked up at Eric and then back down at me, and it started to squash me with its trunk just as Eric hit it again in the same skull area. This area of the skull is nothing more than a fulcrum for the animal to lift its very heavy trunk. Many inexperienced hunters are killed because they think this is the animal's brain. It isn't. Eric knew that the only chance I had was for him to stun the elephant. Killing it would topple two tons of elephant right on top of me. It stumbled about some more before it left to join the other elephants. I must have consumed two gallons of different liquids on the way back to Lusaka. Eric relates what he saw:

> The unmistakable, chilling trumpet of an enraged elephant came from where I had left Brick and Guy. I ran to the Land Rover, grabbed my .458 Winchester, and ran flat out toward the sound, loading as I went...I heard another furious trumpet, and there, about three hundred yards ahead, I saw an elephant chasing a person. I closed in much sooner than I ever thought possible, as they were coming toward me.
>
> Guy could really sprint, but the young bull was fast gaining ground anyway. I fired a shot into the ground just in front of it, which did not slow the charging beast at all. This charge was for real: The bull's ears were squeezed tightly against its body, and its trunk was curled up under its jaw. Time for Guy was running out, and I had only a few seconds to prevent a tragedy.
>
> Guy was about fifty yards from me when he turned around and, in a futile attempt to protect himself, threw his movie camera into the face of his charging adversary. He was knocked down by its outstretched trunk, and the elephant now stood almost on top of Guy, who lay motionless beneath his six-ton attacker. I was now only ten yards or so from the coup de grace, crushing Guy to death and possible impaling him with a tusk. I aimed my rifle at the tiny cavity that protects the football-size brain. In a split second before I pulled the trigger, I realized that a brain shot might well drop the hulk right on top of Guy, probably killing him, so I raised my aimpoint. The elephant's front legs were bending to kneel on Guy. In a split second I raised my aim to place my bullet into the "honeycomb" structure that surrounds the brain. This, in theory, meant that the elephant would fall sideways, sit on its haunches, or collapse forward. I prayed for the latter not to happen. Luckily as my bullet hit the bull, he fell over sideways and then sat on his backside, trumpeting, not knowing what had hit him. I was thankful to see the elephant sit down, much like a boxer getting a solid hit, rather than falling on top of Guy.
>
> The animal was dazed and struggling to regain its feet. Guy was almost knocked out from the terrific blow he had received in his back from the charging elelephant. I shouted, "Get the hell out of there!" Guy just looked at me with glazed eyes and was speechless. I didn't blame him-not many folks have gazed up at an elephant and lived. I ran up and dragged Guy out from under the dazed elephant with one hand, clenching my .458 in the other. How I managed to do this, I will never know, as Guy weighed in the region of 200 pounds. Surely some "Super Power" took over and gave me the strength to enable me to virtually throw Guy out of the way. Then I turned to face the elephant, which had recovered its footing and was going around in circles trying to get oriented. I pulled Guy farther away and had a good look to see how badly injured he was. I thought he might have died from sheer shock. He was at least breathing, although his face was as white as aspirin. The elephant, still wandering around in the general area, gave a gurgled squeal and took off in the opposite direction.

Lake Manyara Lioness, Oil on Canvas

The Post
August 3, 1999

BRITISH STUDENT EATEN BY LIONS IN ZIMBABWE

HARARE, Zimbabwe — A British student was dragged out of his tent by a pride of lions and torn to pieces in a nature reserve in northern Zimbabwe, police and parks officials said Monday. David Pleydell-Bouverie, 18, was with a tour group in the Matusadonha National Park, 300 miles northwest of the capital Harare, when the group of 10-12 lions attacked early Sunday, said police spokesman Wayne Bvudzijena. He was filling in before college as an unpaid helper with a Zimbabwean tour firm. Parks officials said the student and professional safari guide Bradley Fouche were in separate tents away from their tour party when Fouche was awoken by screaming and saw Pleydell-Bouverie being dragged from his tent. The guide set fire to his shirt to try to scare away the lions and by the time he reached his rifle the student had been carried into thick bush nearby. The student's head and other body parts were found in the bush. Rangers later shot two lionesses from the pride that attacked him. Regulations in the park, where lions are common, require visitors to be accompanied at all times by a qualified guide, with a firearm at hand for any emergency.

Thanks for small mercies, I thought, relieved that I didn't have to kill the poor beast. After collecting Stang, Eric got us to the vehicle and we left for Lusaka.

About a year and a half later at the Game Conservation International dinner in San Antonio, Eric gave a speech and we showed the film of mine and the other photographer. It was dramatic to say the least and I was grateful. When I had left Eric at the airport, I asked him what his favorite animal was in Zambia to which he responded, "the kudu." Continues Eric at the dinner:

> *Guy presented me with an original painting of a greater kudu with an inscription that reads, "To Eric Balson, to whom this intrepid, but foolish artist owes his life."*

Yes, I am very much afraid of elephants, and am constantly amazed at my stupidity.

A couple of years later I was staying at the Chobe lodge in Botswana. Pat Carr Hartley, who was managing Hunters Africa at the time, offered to take me for a ride through the Chobe Game Park in an open Land Rover because it afforded better visibility. (Pat once went into a herd of cow and calf elephants with nothing but a chair, mind you. He must have been very swift of feet, but either way he survived that and many other lunatic encounters.) Pat knew I was terrified of elephants but thought I liked living on the edge. This very bad mixture had us tearing away from elephants all afternoon. In Chobe it is very difficult to avoid elephants anyway. Heading back, we surprised a lone cow, which immediately came for us. We barely got away from her because of the deep sand we were in. In the process we ran over some exposed mopane tree roots which apparently caused the whole tree to vibrate because a huge black mamba dropped out of the tree right on my lap. After a few instant slashing bites on the seat, it slithered off into the bush. Mention Pat's name to me and I turn white to this day. We did meet again all too briefly, in 1992, and it was very nice seeing him again.

CONCLUSIONS

Lions used to be culled "to save game." This culling of the lion population, as with most predators, had a limited effect, and the species rapidly replenished itself. The South African game parks are the most intensively managed wild animal populations in Africa. Experiences there in managing both wild land and cattle-grazing priorities do not bode too well for lions and wild game in general, but they have shown that it can be done. The future of those lion populations is secure, and although artificially managed, they are a model for the other areas in Africa.

The Natal Witness

June 22, 1984

A DANISH WOMAN WAS BADLY MAULED BY A LION in Kenya's Aberdare Mountains but saved her baby by dropping him behind her, the Danish embassy confirmed yesterday. The incident occurred on May 20 but was apparently kept quiet by Danish and Kenyan authorities until the victim, identified as Mrs. Helen Karlsen, was evacuated to Copenhagen for further treatment this week. She suffered wounds on her face, neck, head, left shoulder and leg.

The Citizen News
July 27, 1998

GRIM SEARCH STILL ON AFTER LIONS DEVOUR FAMILY

Kruger National Park rangers are still searching for the remains of a Mozambican family who were reportedly attacked and devoured by a pride of lions while attempting to cross into South Africa through the northern section of the park. The search was sparked by the discovery last Wednesday of a dazed young Mozambican girl wandering in the park after she allegedly spent last Tuesday night in an ant-bear hole while the lions attacked her family. Kruger Park director David Mabunda confirmed the attack, saying the girl had told rangers that when she crawled out of the hole the next morning all she found left of her family was her mother's head. "She heard screams and growls and spent the night in the hole. The next morning she went back. All she could find was her mother's head," said Mr. Mabunda. He said trail ranger Nick Squires found the girl wandering alone in the veld and took her to the camp at Punda Maria. A search that afternoon recovered the family's luggage at the scene, where blood was found on the ground.

"Lions had apparently attacked the luggage; there were no drag marks or signs of other possible mortalities and the search had to be called off due to poor light," added Mr. Mabunda. He said a second search last Thursday revealed the tracks of two children who appeared to have followed a powerline back to Mozambique. The girl is receiving medical attention and counseling. Mr. Mabunda declined to say where she was being kept. The family were apparently trying to cross illegally into South Africa from Mozambique when the attack happened. — African Eye News Service

The Citizen
January 4, 1993

ZOO LIONS MAUL THIEF TO DEATH IN NAMIBIA

WINDHOEK — Lions mauled to death a thief who broke into a zoo in Namibia to steal mangoes. The lions were let out of their enclosure at night to deter would-be thieves from crossing perimeter fences, said Joe Bradley, a keeper at Ekongoro Zoo. They were sitting next to the corpse of 20-year-old Lucas Tileni when officials opened the zoo on Sunday morning, he said. Tileni crossed a 3.5 metre double fence and a ditch to get into the zoo. Police said local magistrates would decide any action against the lions or the zoo. Mr. Bradley said he "reared the lions from cubs and they were tame as pet dogs."

One thing I think most all agree on is that the reintroduction of captive lions in Africa makes no sense at all. It achieves nothing. Unlike transferring wild lions from one area to another, the genes of captive-bred lions have not been run through the gauntlet of nature's natural selection process. More than likely, these ill-equipped lions will die a much crueler death than if left in captivity. I suppose a case could be made for the reintroduction of the Asian lion in the Gir Forest in India. But with so little land and such a small gene pool, that is a situation that certainly looks grim.

When Pat Hepburn, who had been warden at Chobe National Park since its inception, left the game department and joined Hunters Africa, he was asked to do a buffalo count along the Savuti channel. Between the western boundary of the Chobe park and the Kwando River he counted 18,000 buffalo. I had the good fortune to have been in the middle of many of those herds. When John Northcote left in 1993, the only buffalo in the whole of this area was a small herd of about sixty. The human population explosion is eliminating many of Africa's animals.

For an insight as to how it once was in most of Africa, read Bill York's experience near the Ethiopian border. He witnessed this narrow belt of surprising lushness.

> *It was about five miles wide and obviously caused by a heavy thunderstorm that had swept through some time before. The topography often acted as a channel, so it was not unusual for heavy deluges to move along a narrow front. When this happened, the resultant verdant growth attracted a large number of wild animals. This strip was thickly populated with every species known to southern Sudan. Large herds of buffalo, elephant, eland, and sizable groups of greater kudu and waterbuck were most in evidence, but other species were prominent as well.*
> *Lack of human pressure meant that these animals were not at all nervous about our presence; we wandered through them with no let or hindrance, some of them merely moving aside and watching us as we passed. In such an animal nirvana it would have been sacrilegious to fire a rifle. I passed on peacefully to less green pastures. Never since, not even in the great national parks of East Africa, have I seen animals so unafraid. Even the numerous lions and leopards dotted about causing scarcely a ripple.*

East Africa has the highest rate of human population increase in the world. Its population doubles approximately every twenty years. In 1967, on my first visit to Amboseli, the entrance was marked only by a wooden sign on a dusty dirt road. Today its approach is by a two lane tarmac road with thousands of beggars and little tourist shops at its border. The normally nomadic elephants which are now confined there have taken what was once a beautiful lush landscape and made a desert of it. They have over-browsed the available food supply in their relatively small sanctuary. Against this, and the resultant growing human demand for food, firewood, and living space, the future of wildlife outside such conservation areas is even more grim.

But for me, Africa has a call that is very hard to ignore. On my second trip there I almost felt I was coming to my real home. Perhaps I'm the reincarnation of some local African, if not A.J. Siggins. He spent most of his adult life in Africa when it was far less comfortable than it is today. "

> "My friends often asked me to leave for a trip home or the south, anywhere for a change, they thought I needed it. But I could no more have left Africa than I could have flown."

I'm a product of New York. I have been immersed in its culture all my life. Lincoln Center, Broadway, the great museums, world championship sports and great restaurants, one of the great cultural centers in the world. But ah, how wonderful it is to be watching lions on the plains of Africa or Kuota moto, Swahili for "dreaming the fire," on an African evening.

BIBLIOGRAPHY

Adamson, G. "Observations on Lions in Serengeti National Park," *East African Wildlife Journal* 2:160–61. 1964

Adamson, J. *Born Free*. Collins, London, 1960

Adamson, J. *Living Free*. Collins, London, 1961

Akeley, C. and M. Akeley, *Lions, Gorillas and Their Neighbors*. Dodd, Mead and Co., New York, 1932

Akeley, Carl E. "Lion Spearing," Special Zoology Leaflet Number 1. Field Museum of Natural History, Chicago, 1926

Arbuthnot, Thomas S. *African Hunt*. W.W. Norton & Co., Inc, New York, 1954

Bartlett, Fred. *Shoot Straight and Stay Alive*. Trophy Room Books, Agoura, CA, 1994

Bonner R. *At the Hand of Man*. Alfred A. Knopf. New York 1993

Carr, Norman. *Kakuli*. CBC Pub., Harare, Zimbabwe ISBN# 0-797-1578-5

Chalmers, Patrick R. *Sport & Travel In East Africa*, E.P. Dutton & Co., New York, 1928 & 1930

Clarke, James L. *Trails of the Hunted*. Little, Brown, and Company, Boston, 1928

Clark, James. *Man is the Prey*. Stein and Day Publishers, New York, 1969

Coheleach, Guy, and Nancy Neff. *The Big Cats: The Paintings of Guy Coheleach*. Harry Abrams, Inc., New York, 1982

Collins, Douglas. *Another Tear For Africa*. Amwell Press, Clinton, New Jersey, 1981

Cowie, M. *The African Lion*. Golden Press, New York, 1966

Crandall, L. *The Management of Wild Mammals in Captivity*. University of Chicago Press, Chicago, 1964

Denis, A. *Cats of the World*. Constable and Co., London, 1964

Dyer, Anthony. *Classic African Animals: The Big Five*. Winchester Press, New York, 1973

Estes, R. "Predators and Scavengers." Natural History 76(2):20–29; 76(3):38-47, 1967

Fosbrooke, H. "An Administrative Survey of the Masai Social System." *Tanzania Notes and Records*, 26:1–50, 1948.

Guggisberg, C. *Simba*. Howard Timmins, Capetown, 1961

Hartley, Lionel A. H. *Hunter's Heartbeat*. Amwell Press, Clinton, New Jersey, 1985

Hemsing, Jan. *Encounters with Lions*. Trophy Room Books, Agoura, CA, 1994

Henley, Tony. *Round the Campfire*. Amwell Press, Clinton, New Jersey, 1989

Herne, Brian. *Tanzania Safaris*. Amwell Press, Clinton, New Jersey, 1981

Hibben, Frank C. *Hunting In Africa*. Hill And Wang, New York, 1962

Howell, A. *Speed in Animals*. University of Chicago Press, Chicago, 1944

Hunter, J.A. *Hunter*. Harper & Brothers, New York, 1952

Hurt, Robin. Letter to Guy Coheleach from Kenya. May 16, 1998

Johnson, M. *Lion*. G.P. Putnam's Sons, New York, 1929

Johnson, Martin. *Safari*. G.P. Putnam's Sons, New York, 1928

Jordan, John Alfred. (as told to John Prebble) *Elephants and Ivory*. HoltRinehart & Company, Inc., New York, 1956

Kaniut, Larry. *Alaska Bear Tales*. Alaska Northwest Books Seattle, Washington. First published by Sammamish Press, 1989

Kaniut, Larry. *More Alaska Bear Tales*. Alaska Northwest Books, Seattle, Washington. First published by Sammamish Press, 1989

Kruuk, H., and M. Turner. "Comparative Notes on Predation by Lion, Leopard, Cheetah and Wild Dog in the Serengeti Area." East Africa *Mammalia*, 31(1):1–27, 1967

Lindstrom, Soren. *Hunting the African Lion*. Amwell Press, Clinton, New Jersey, 1989

Lyell, Denis D. *Big Game Shooting in Africa*. Maydon, Seeley, Service & Co., London, 1957

Makacha, S., and G. Schaller. "Observations on Lions in the Lake Manyara National Park, Tanzania." *East African Wildlife Journal*, 7:99–103, 1969

Mangani, B. "Buffalo Kills Lion." *African Wild Life*, 16(1):27, 1962

Markham, Beryl. *West with the Night*. North Point Press, San Francisco, 1983

McBride, Chris. *The White Lions of Timbavati*. Paddington Press, Ltd., New York and London, 1977

Meinertzhagen. *Kenya Diary* 1902–1906. Oliver & Boyd, 1957

Northcote, John. *From Sailor to Professional Hunter*. Trophy Room Books, Agoura, CA. 1997

Omanney, David. *Hunting the African Lion*. Amwell Press, Clinton, New Jersey, 1989

Owens, Mark & Delia. *Cry of the Kalahari*. Houghton Mifflin Co., 1984; *The Eye of the Elephant*. Houghton Mifflin Co., 1992

Packer, Craig. *Into Africa*. The University Of Chicago Press, Chicago, 1994

Patterson, J.H. *The Man-Eaters of Tsavo*. Macmillan Company, New York, 1927

Pease, A. *The Book of the Lion*. John Murray, London, 1914

Percival, A. *A Game Ranger's Note Book*. Nisbet and Co., London, 1924

Player, Ian. *Zulu Wilderness*. Fulcrum Publishing, Golden, Colorado, 1998

Rainsford, W. *The Land of the Lion*. Doubleday, New York, 1909

Rikhoff, James. *Hunting the African Lion*. Amwell Press, Clinton, New Jersey, 1989

Roosevelt, T. and E. Heller. *Life Histories of African Game Animals*, Volume 1. John Murray, London,1922

Roosevelt, Theodore. *African Game Trails*. Charles Scribner's Sons, New York, 1910

Sadleir, R. "Notes on Reproduction in the Larger Felidae," *International Zoo Yearbook*, Volume 6. Zoological Society, London, 1966

Schaller, G. "Life with the King of Beasts." *National Geographic*, 135(4):494–519, 1969

Schaller, George B. *The Serengeti Lion*. The Chicago University Press, Chicago & London, 1972

Schaller, George B. *Serengeti, A Kingdom of Predators*. The Chicago University Press, Chicago & London, 1973

Selous, F. *African Nature Notes and Reminiscences*. Macmillan, London, 1908

Selous, Frederick C. *A Hunter's Wanderings in Africa*. Richard Bentley & Sons, London, 1890

Seth-Smith Tony. For the Honour of A Hunter... Trophy Room Books, Agoura, CA. 1996

Siggins, A.J. *Man-Killers I Have Known*. Trophy Room Books, Agoura, CA 1988.

Simon, N. "Red Data Book, Volume 1." *Mammalia* IUCN, Morges, Switzerland, 1966

Smuts, Anderson, and Austin. "Age Determination of the African Lion (*Panthera Leo*)," *Journal Zoology Land*, 1978

Stevenson-Hamilton, J. *Wild Life in South Africa*. Cassell, London, 1954

Stevenson-Hamilton, J. Colonel Stevenson. *Big Game Shooting In Africa*. Maydon, Seeley, Service & Co., Ltd., London 28(1): 815-27, 1964

Talbot, L,. and D. Stewart. "First Wildlife Census of the Entire Serengeti-Mara Region, East Africa." *Journal of Wildlife Management*, 28(1): 815–27, 1964

Taylor, John. *African Rifles and Cartridges*. Gun Room Press, Highland Park, New Jersey, 1977

Turner, M. "Tanzania's Serengeti." *Africana*, 2(5):11–18, 1965

von Blixen-Finecke, Bror. *African Hunter*. Alfred A. Knopf, New York, 1938

Watson, R. and M Turner. "A Count of the Large Mammals of the Lake Manyara National Park: Results and Discussion." *East African Wildlife Journal*, 3:95–98, 1965

Wells, E. *Lions Wild and Friendly*. Viking Press, New York, 1934

Wolhuter, Harry. *Memories of a Game Ranger*. The Wildlife Protection Society of South Africa, Johannesburg, 1948

Wright, B. "Predation on Big Game in East Africa." *Journal of Wildlife Management*, 24(1):1–15, 1960

York, William. *Out in the Midday Shade*. Safari Press, Long Beach, CA, 2000

Zaidle, Don. *American Man-Killers*. Safari Press, Long Beach, CA, 1997

Zuckerman, S. "The Breeding Season of Mammals in Captivity." *Proceedings of the Zoological Society*, London, 122(1):827–950, 1953